The Cambridge Manuals of Science and Literature

THE ICELANDIC SAGAS

CAMBRIDGE UNIVERSITY PRESS
London: FETTER LANE, E.C.
C. F. CLAY, Manager

Edinburgh: 100, PRINCES STREET
Berlin: A. ASHER AND CO.
Leipzig: F. A. BROCKHAUS
New York: G. P. PUTNAM'S SONS
Bombay and Calcutta: MACMILLAN AND CO., LTD.

All rights reserved

THE ICELANDIC SAGAS

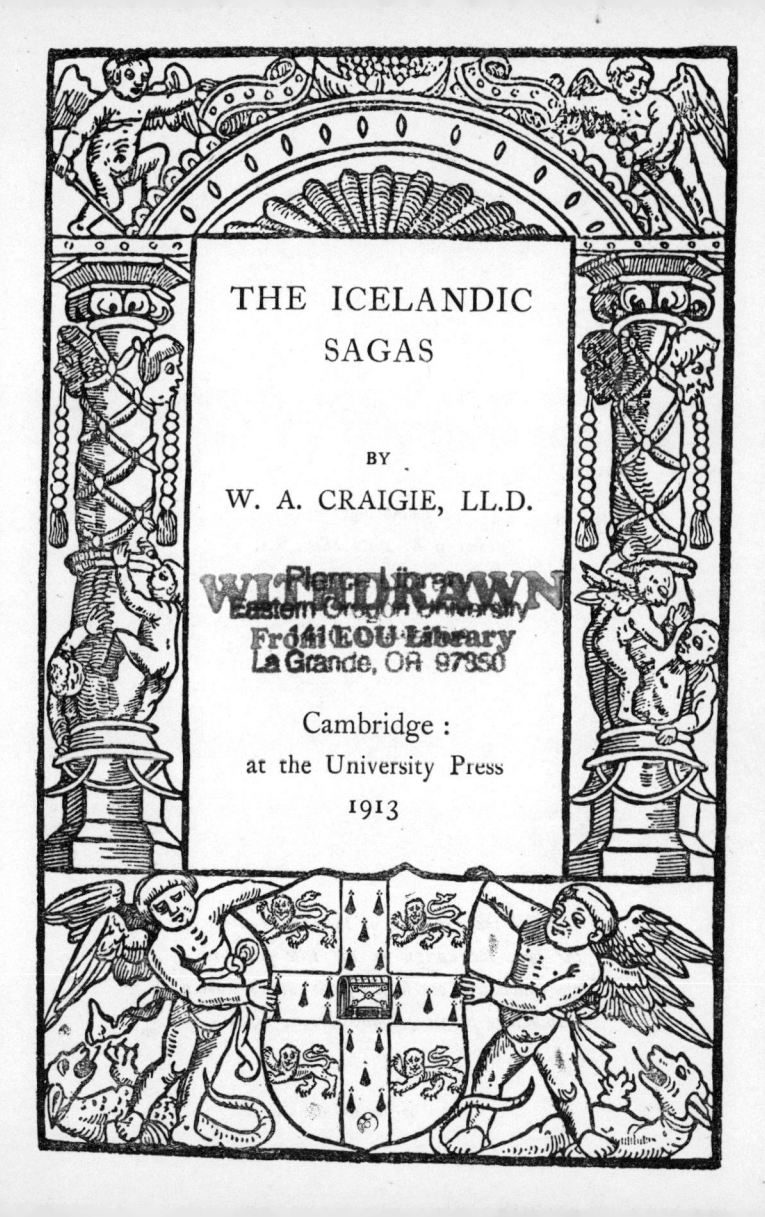

BY

W. A. CRAIGIE, LL.D.

Cambridge:
at the University Press
1913

Cambridge:
PRINTED BY JOHN CLAY, M.A.
AT THE UNIVERSITY PRESS

With the exception of the coat of arms at the foot, the design on the title page is a reproduction of one used by the earliest known Cambridge printer, John Siberch, 1521

PRINTED IN GREAT BRITAIN

PREFACE

IN this brief outline of an extensive subject I have endeavoured to explain clearly not only what the Icelandic sagas are, but how it happened that they arose in a place so remote from the rest of Europe. This is certainly one of the most surprising features of this unique literature, though in reality it is not quite so strange as it appears. The special reasons which explain it are fully stated in the first chapter, but there is also a general consideration which perhaps ought not to be overlooked. In respect of early original literature, the central Germanic area is not strongly represented; it is on the outmost borders, in Iceland, England, and southern Germany, that literary activity of a high order first manifests itself. This would appear to suggest that the Germanic race was first enabled to create original literature of a permanent character when it had come into contact with, or even had largely mixed with, other races, and had received the impulse of new experiences.

Thus the more central peoples of the Germanic stock—the southern Scandinavians, the Frisians, the Saxons, and the Lower Franks—have either little or nothing in the way of early literature to set beside the poetry and prose of the extreme north, west, and south. However this may be, the cultivation of a great poetic and prose literature in Iceland is remarkable enough, and becomes more notable when the period to which it belongs is considered. The poetry, so far as preserved, dates from about or before 900, and is very copious for the centuries that follow. The prose literature begins about 1120, and is at its highest level in the thirteenth century, at a time when there was practically no writing of prose either in England or in Germany. The comparative isolation of Iceland enabled it to take its own course, and to preserve, in its own language and with its own literary style, the records of its own past and of other countries as well.

It is one peculiarity of this style that it makes little or no distinction between fact and fiction; in either case there is the same minuteness of detail and the same apparent good faith or implicit belief on the part of the narrator. This feature is apt to be misunderstood, especially in the earlier stages of saga-reading, and I have specially endeavoured to show clearly the real facts of the matter.

With regard to the Icelandic names of persons and titles of sagas occurring throughout the book, the only points to be noted are that vowels marked with an acute accent are long, that *j* has the value of the semi-vowel *y*, and that the letter ð represents the soft or voiced *th*, as in *bathe*. In translations of the sagas and other works it is commonly expressed by a simple *d*, as in Odin, Sigurd.

W. A. CRAIGIE.

OXFORD,
November, 1912.

CONTENTS

CHAP.		PAGE
	PREFACE	v
I.	THE ORIGIN OF THE SAGAS	1
II.	THE WRITTEN SAGA	19
III.	HISTORICAL SAGAS RELATING TO ICELAND AND GREENLAND	34

§ i. The shorter sagas.
§ ii. The longer sagas.
§ iii. Ecclesiastical sagas.
§ iv. Sagas of later times.

IV.	HISTORICAL SAGAS RELATING TO NORWAY AND OTHER NORTHERN LANDS	79
V.	MYTHICAL AND ROMANTIC SAGAS	92
VI.	SAGAS FROM LATIN SOURCES	104
VII.	ENGLISH TRANSLATIONS AND OTHER AIDS . .	110
	INDEX	117

ILLUSTRATIONS AND MAP

PLATE		
I.	Part of *Njáls Saga* . . .	to face page 68
II.	Part of *Orkneyinga Saga* . .	to face page 88
Iceland (showing the saga-districts) . .		at end of book

CHAPTER I

THE ORIGIN OF THE SAGAS

The general title of *Icelandic Sagas* is used to denote a very extensive body of prose literature written in Iceland, and in the language of that country, at various dates between the middle of the twelfth century and the beginning of the fifteenth; the end of the period, however, is less clearly marked than the beginning. The common feature of the works classed under this name, which vary greatly in length, value, and interest, is that they have the outward form of historical or biographical narratives; but the matter is often purely fictitious, and in many cases fact and fiction are inseparably blended. Both in the form and in the matter there is much that is conventional, and many features of style and content are quite peculiar to the special Icelandic mode of story-telling.

The word *saga* (of which the plural is *sögur*) literally means 'something said,' and was in use long before there was any written literature in Iceland. From an early period it had been a custom, which in course of time became an accomplishment and an art, to put together in a connected form the exploits of some notable man or the record of some memorable event, and to relate the story thus composed as a means of entertainment and instruction. It was out of these oral narratives, augmented and elaborated during the course of several centuries, that the written saga finally arose; but before entering into any account of how this came to pass it will be well to explain why Iceland, of all the Scandinavian countries, became the home of this form of literature. For this purpose it is necessary to take a brief survey of the history of that island, and of its relations with the lands lying nearest to it.

Iceland was colonized, mainly from Norway, and almost entirely by settlers of Norwegian origin, during the half-century or so following upon the year 874 A.D. As late as the middle of the ninth century, Norway was still a country of small kingdoms, each independent of the other, and having distinctive names. Even within these petty kingdoms the power of the kings was far from absolute, and many earls and chiefs were men of as much importance and influence as some of those who bore the royal name. The Viking period, with its constant expeditions to foreign lands in search of plunder, fostered the spirit of independence by enriching the bolder spirits of the community, and made them less inclined than ever to brook interference from those of higher rank. With the second half of the century an important change took place. Harald the Fairhaired, whose paternal kingdom was limited to a small district in the east of Norway, began at an early age to extend his domain by conquest. According to the story given in the saga of Harald, his desire of dominion was mainly due to the words of a girl, who refused to consider his wooing of her so long as he was only king over a few small districts; "and I think it strange," she said, "that there is no king who will try to make Norway his own, as Gorm has done in Denmark, and Eirík at Uppsala." When these words were reported to Harald, he declared himself grateful for them, and made a vow never to cut or comb his hair, until he had made himself master of the whole of Norway. The following years, from 865 onwards, witnessed the rapid fulfilment of this resolve, culminating in the great sea-fight at Hafrsfirth on the west coast of Norway, in the year 872. After this battle, says his saga, King Harald met with no further resistance. His greatest opponents had either fallen, or fled from the country; and the latter were sufficiently numerous to colonize several new districts, such as Jamtaland and Helsingland (in modern Sweden), and even new-found lands like the Færöes and Iceland. There was also much emigration to Shetland; and many powerful men who were outlawed by Harald took to 'western viking.' They lived in the Orkneys or the Hebrides in the winter, while in the summer they plundered in Norway, and did much damage there.

The tendency to make the British Isles their chief resort, on the part of those who could not or would not remain in Norway after Harald's triumph, was greatly checked by the discovery of Iceland. As soon as the existence of this extensive island (larger even than Ireland) became generally known, and some idea had been gained of what it could offer to the settler, one or two of the bolder spirits were not long in seizing the opportunity which thus presented itself. The land was to be had for the taking, for the only inhabitants were a few Celtic monks who had wandered there in quest of solitude and who left again when the new settlers came; and the long sea-voyage did not deter men to whom the sea had become almost a second home. The first settlement, that of Ingólf, appears to have taken place in 874, and for the next fifty or sixty years a steady stream of colonists, coming either directly from Norway or from the Norwegian settlements in Britain, poured into the island, until every valley round its deeply indented coast had been occupied. So great was the emigration from Norway that King Harald became alarmed, and tried to lessen it by imposing a tax on every one who went out to Iceland. Thanks to the deep and unbroken interest in genealogy and history among subsequent generations of Icelanders, a very full record of the details

of the colonization has been preserved, and is to be
found in the compilation known as *Landnáma-bók*,
while the broader outlines are carefully stated in the
still earlier *Íslendinga-bók* of Ari the Learned. From
these two works, as well as from many of the sagas,
the names and much of the history of all the leading
settlers are known; and it is thus possible to understand clearly both their relations with their old home
and the manner in which they adapted themselves to
their new one.

Not a few of these settlers belonged to old and
famous families in Norway, and some of them were
closely connected with kings and earls there, or in
other Scandinavian countries. When these removed
to Iceland, they were accompanied by many of their
adherents and dependents, and asserted for themselves
in the new land the leading place they had held in the
old. To such settlers it was a source of pride to recall
and recount the names and exploits of the famous men
to whom they were related; and an immense quantity
of old lore, reaching back into early prehistoric times,
was thus carried out to Iceland, and preserved there
after it had been forgotten in the place of its origin.
Not a few of these men had also seen much of other
lands before they went to end their days in Iceland.
Some had played an active part as vikings—to them
an honourable as well as profitable occupation—and
had plundered in the Baltic lands, or in the British

Isles, or even further south. Others had seen the manners and men of foreign countries in the more peaceful capacity of traders, and as such had frequented not only foreign towns but even the courts of foreign kings, as Ohthere and Wulfstan did that of King Alfred. Others again, as we have already seen, had been actually settled for some time in the Scottish islands, or in Ireland, and had intermarried with the Gaelic peoples there. Some of these were men and women of great distinction, and played a prominent part in the early history of Iceland, though their number was smaller than has sometimes been supposed; at the very most only one in every six of the leading settlers came from 'west the sea.' Many of these colonists brought with them thralls belonging to other countries, some of whom were almost immediately set free and established in homes of their own, thus helping towards a mixture of race which can be clearly observed at the present day. In all this there was much matter worthy of being remembered, and the origin and adventures of such men formed themes of great interest both for their own descendants and for others.

As might be expected, the occupation of a new land by this crowd of strong-willed men, already taught by experience how to hold their own against others, did not always take place in a peaceful manner. There were some who recognized no right as prior to their own, and did not hesitate to make their own strong arm the law. Quarrels readily arose over small matters, and northern ideas as to the duty of revenge often converted these differences into prolonged and bitter family feuds with violent and tragic endings. Out of these many conflicts between persons and families there grew fresh matter for tradition, and in each district the memory of notable men and their deeds of courage or mischief was long and carefully preserved. This preservation was greatly assisted by a strong bent towards the art of story-telling, which often led to the incidents being narrated in good set form by one or other of the parties concerned, while they were still new and capable of being verified. The story thus told was then carefully learned by others, and handed on with all its details, in a way that would have been impossible with any looser or less formal style of tradition. The accuracy of the narrative was often further secured by another factor—the Icelandic fondness for poetry. In many cases the events had been the cause or theme of single verses or of poems, whether composed by actors in the affair or by others, and these not only served to adorn the tale, but could be cited to prove the facts. In another line of tradition, as will presently be seen, such verses and poems were of even greater value.

Although isolated by their position in a remote island of the Atlantic, the Icelanders did not allow themselves to become a secluded people, with no interest in the lands beyond the sea and no knowledge of their affairs. For several generations close relations were maintained not only with their original home in Norway, but also with Sweden, Denmark, and the British Isles. Apart from the risks involved in crossing the wide stretch of ocean, risks which were reduced as far as possible by sailing only in summer, there was no difficulty in keeping up an intimate connexion with these countries. The Icelander, in fact, had exceptional qualifications for doing so. He spoke a language which at the beginning of the eleventh century was still in use over the whole of Scandinavia and in part of Russia, which had also extended its range to the north and west of Scotland, to the north and east of England, to the chief sea-ports in Ireland, and even to the greater part of Normandy. Over the whole of this great area, with its complex nationalities, its varied culture, and rapidly changing history, the Icelander could range with little difficulty, and converse with men of his own tongue. If he were still more adventurous, he could make his way down the great Russian rivers and so reach the court of the Byzantine Emperor, whose bodyguard he would find composed of men of his own race and speech. Many Icelanders did avail themselves of these opportunities, and everywhere met with the most encouraging reception. Their reputation in general stood very high, either as good and faithful fighting-men, honest and enterprising merchants, or skilful poets and story-tellers. In Scandinavia and the British Isles they were usually welcome at the courts of kings and earls, and many of them obtained high positions of trust under these, or received from them special marks of favour or esteem.

These exceptional opportunities of acquiring information about foreign lands were not neglected. The Icelander who went abroad, and sooner or later returned home, brought back with him a well-filled budget of instructive or entertaining matter, which he soon communicated to eager ears and retentive memories. The information thus gained might have quickly spread from man to man by means of ordinary intercourse, but its diffusion was further assisted in no small degree by special circumstances. Within a short time after the settlement began, local assemblies (called *things*) had grown up in various parts of the island, and formed regular meeting places for all the men of the district. Later on, in the year 930, a general assembly for the whole country (the *Althingi*) was established, and met every year in the tenth week of summer for the transaction of legislative and legal business. The local gatherings were also regulated, and were held annually in spring and autumn. Both the smaller and the greater assemblies formed natural centres for the exchange of the latest news,

Icelandic and foreign, and the opportunities they afforded were fully taken advantage of. Those who had an interest in such matters took care to learn all they could from the newly returned voyagers, and by doing so year after year gradually acquired a store of knowledge relating to the history of the neighbouring countries and their great men. This they put together in the best form they could; and the narrative as told by them was learned by others, and so handed on to later times. It is to these instinctive historians, whose diligence in collecting the facts was equalled by their power of remembering and skill in recounting them, that we owe practically all our knowledge of Scandinavian history prior to the twelfth century, together with much that throws light on the early history of the British Isles.

This branch of historical tradition also gained immensely in fulness and accuracy by the existence of a large body of poetry which was closely connected with it. This partly consisted of single verses called forth by particular incidents, as in the case of the purely Icelandic traditions already mentioned, but also included a large number of shorter or longer poems, in which the exploits of some king or earl were celebrated. From an early period it had been a regular practice among the poets in Norway to recommend themselves to the notice of some noble patron by a poem of this kind, and many poets enjoyed the special favour of the great man to whom they attached themselves. In the second half of the tenth century the art of poetry began to decline in Norway itself, and thenceforward, with few exceptions, it was by Icelanders only that the profession of *skáld* was followed. For the young Icelander, going abroad for the first time, one of the surest ways to attract attention, and lay the foundations of his fortune, was to have his poem ready when he arrived at the residence of the king or earl whom he visited, and obtain permission to recite it as soon as possible. This first poem was necessarily based upon information which he had collected in Iceland, but his subsequent work often recorded only what he had seen with his own eyes, as he followed his liege-lord by sea and land and took part in his battles. The number of such poets during the tenth and eleventh centuries was very great, and their poems were naturally still more numerous. Their importance as historical evidence is strongly emphasized by the great Icelandic historian, Snorri Sturluson, in the prologue to his *Heimskringla*, written about 1225. "There were skalds with Harald (the Fairhaired)," he says, "and men still know their poems, and the poems about all the kings who have since ruled in Norway. And we take our statements most of all from what is said in those poems which were recited before the rulers themselves or their sons. We accept as true all that is found in these about their exploits or battles. It is certainly the custom of poets to praise most highly the person they are addressing, but no one would have dared to recite to the man himself exploits which he and all the hearers knew to be false and feigned; that would have been mockery and not praise." Although the poems thus referred to by Snorri mainly relate to Norwegian kings, many of the events recounted in them bore upon the history of the other Scandinavian countries and the British Isles. Moreover, there were also Icelandic poets who made their way to Sweden and Denmark, to the Orkneys, to Ireland, and even to the English court, and composed poems in which they recounted the exploits of the kings and earls whom they found there. These poems, no less than the others, were in due time carried back to Iceland, and helped to maintain and increase a knowledge of the affairs of these countries. The total number of such poems known and repeated in Iceland during the eleventh and twelfth centuries must have been very great. It is recorded of one man, Stúf the Blind, who was himself a poet, that he could recite more than thirty long encomia (called *drápur*) and as many shorter ones (*flokkar*); this was about the year 1060.

Out of all these materials there gradually grew up in Iceland a rich body of genuine historical tradition, beginning from at least the days of King Harald and the settlement of the island, and becoming fuller and more accurate in proportion as the events were more recent. To know as much of this as possible, and to be able to relate it in an interesting way, was an object of ambition to many Icelanders, whose fame as saga-men came in time to equal their reputation as poets. For mere entertainment, however, it was not necessary that the narrative should be strictly historical or perfectly in accordance with fact; fiction also had its admirers and cultivators, and legend was no less in demand than veracious history or biography. The stages by which this species of saga-telling developed are by no means clear, but its beginnings were probably very early. Among its favourite subjects were persons and incidents belonging to early periods, from which only vague traditions had been preserved; here the fancy of the narrator had free scope, and troubled itself very little as to whether the incidents were probable or even possible. Unfortunately this type of saga tended to encroach upon and vitiate the other; fictitious elements came to be introduced into genuine traditions, and often in such a manner that it was no longer possible to separate the one from the other. This feature of the sagas may easily be misunderstood, and the fact has not always been sufficiently recognized that deliberate invention had its share in the work, and is the source of much that might seem to indicate an uncritical tradition or ignorant credulity.

That saga-telling was one of the chief modes of entertainment among the Icelanders of this period would be sufficiently evident from the mass of traditional matter preserved in the written literature of the twelfth and thirteenth centuries. In the sagas themselves, however, the practice is frequently mentioned, and some of the more interesting passages may be cited here to complete the outlines given in the preceding pages. When Thormóð the poet was in Greenland, where he had gone with the object of avenging his foster-brother Thorgeir, he one day went to sleep in the booth (one of the temporary dwellings used by those who attended the *thing* or assembly). On waking up, he found the place empty. Then one came in and said, "You are too far away from a great entertainment." Thormóð asked, "Where have you come from, and what pastime is going on?" Egil answered, "I was at Thorgrím's booth, and nearly the whole assembly is there now." Thormóð asked, "What pastime have they there?" Egil said, "Thorgrím is telling a saga." Thormóð said, "About whom is the saga that he tells?" Egil answered, "I do not know clearly about whom it is; but I know that he tells it well, and in an entertaining manner. He is seated on a chair outside his booth, and the people are sitting round about him and listening to the saga." Thormóð said, "You must be able to give the name of some man who comes into the saga, especially as you speak so highly of it." Egil said, "A certain Thorgeir was a great hero in the saga; and it seems to me that Thorgrím himself must have taken some part in it, and borne himself bravely, as might be expected. I would like you to go there and listen to the entertainment." (That Egil did not know more about the story is explained by the fact that he was but half-witted.)

In the saga of Njál it is told that when Kári and his comrades landed in the Orkneys on Christmas Day, and went up to the hall of Earl Sigurd, they found Gunnar Lambason in the act of telling how Njál's homestead and its inmates were burned by Flosi and his associates. Gunnar, who had also taken a part in the burning, was seated on a chair in front of King Sigtrygg of Dublin, and all the seats in the hall were filled with hearers. As Kári and the others stood listening outside, King Sigtrygg asked, "How did Skarp-heðin stand the burning?" "Well at first," said Gunnar, "but in the end he wept," and all through the story he told much both unfairly and falsely. Kári could not stand this, sprang in with drawn sword, and swept off Gunnar's head in a moment.

How an untravelled Icelander could learn about events that took place in other lands is well illustrated by the story of a young man, who came one summer to the court of King Harald (surnamed *harðráði*), and was received there on condition that he should tell sagas whenever he was required to do so. When Christmas came near, the Icelander showed signs of dejection. The king suspected that this was because his sagas had come to an end, and he had no entertainment to offer during the festive season. The Icelander admitted that this was really the case. "I have only one saga left," he said, "and I dare not tell that here, for it is about your own adventures in foreign lands." "That is the saga I should most of all like to hear," said the king, and gave him directions how to make it last over the Christmas festival. The king's men knew nothing of this arrangement, and many of them thought it a piece of great presumption on the part of the Icelander, and wondered how the king would take it. The king, however, showed no sign either way. On the twelfth day the saga was finished, and on the thirteenth the king said, "Are you not curious, Icelander, to know how I am pleased with the saga?" "I am rather afraid about that," was the reply. "I like it very well," said the king, "who taught it to you?" He answered, "It was my custom in Iceland to go every summer to the Thing, and each summer I learned part of the saga from Halldór Snorrason." "Then it is not remarkable that you know it so well," said the king. Halldór was another Icelander, who had been with Harald while he fought for the Greek emperor in Greece, Africa, and Italy, and afterwards carried home the story of all his exploits in these lands.

The use of saga-telling to enliven festive gatherings is further illustrated in the account of a wedding, which took place at Reykhólar (in the north-west of Iceland) in the year 1119. "Hrólf of Skálmarness," it says, "told the saga about Hröngviđ the viking, and Ólaf, king of the Lithsmen, and the breaking into the grave-mound of Thráin the berserk, and Hrómund Gripsson, and many verses along with it. With this saga King Sverrir was entertained, and he said that such lying sagas were the most entertaining of all; and yet some men trace their descent from Hrómund Gripsson. Hrólf had put this saga together himself.—Ingimund the priest told the saga of Orm, the poet of Barrey, with many verses in it, and at the end of it a good poem which Ingimund had composed; and for that reason many learned men take this saga as true." This passage is of great interest and value, as evidence not only for the personal authorship of these fictitious sagas, but for the fact that their unhistorical character was quite well understood.

The incident just described took place at the time when a written literature was about to arise in Iceland. Yet so strong was the interest in hearing stories told by good narrators, that the art was still in high favour a century and a half later. When Sturla the historian visited Norway in 1263, he accompanied King Magnus on board ship, and sailed south along the coast with him. In the evening, when men lay down to sleep, Sturla was asked to entertain them. Thereupon he told the saga of the witch-woman Huld, and related it much better than any of the listeners had ever heard it told before. Many then crowded forward on the deck to hear the story as well as possible, until there was a great throng there. The queen asked, "What is that crowd forward on the deck there?" One replied, "It is men who want to hear the saga that the Icelander is telling." She said, "What saga is that?" He answered, "It is about a great troll-wife, and it is a good saga, and moreover it is well told." Next day the queen sent for Sturla, and bade him come to her, "and bring with him the saga of the troll-wife." She then asked him to tell the story over again, and he did so during a great part of the day. When he had finished, the queen and many others thanked him, and looked upon him as a learned and clever man. Not long after this, King Magnus gave to Sturla the task of putting together the saga of his father, King Hákon, according to information supplied by the best authorities. Sturla not only did this, but wrote the saga of King Magnus as well.

CHAPTER II

THE WRITTEN SAGA

So far we have considered the Icelandic sagas in their original form of stories or oral accounts, told by skilled narrators as a means of instruction or entertainment. It was long before any attempt was made to convert these into written narratives, and thus produce a literature in the ordinary sense of the word. Although the use of letters (in the form known as *runes*) had been known in Scandinavia from a very early period, there had been no practice of employing them on such an extensive scale as would have been involved in recording a saga, or even a poem. They were used for short inscriptions on stones or articles of metal, or for short messages cut on wooden staves, but there is no evidence that anyone had thought of using them in connexion with pen, ink, and parchment. The suggestion for this use of letters came from without, from the south, along with another change of great importance.

In the year 1000, after a stubborn but short resistance on the part of those who favoured the old faith, Christianity was formally adopted by law as the religion of Iceland. This in time naturally brought with it the culture of the mediæval church, and a knowledge of Latin. Many of the leading Icelanders began to take a great interest in the new learning with which they were thus brought into contact, and became diligent students of the ecclesiastical and secular literature which they found written in the language of the church. Not a few of them studied sufficiently to be ordained as priests, even although they never became real ecclesiastics, nor in any way gave up their temporal position and authority. Fortunately the new learning did not push out the old; the interest in saga-themes continued to be as strong as ever, and in some respects was even strengthened by the fresh sources of information which reading now opened up. Even the old mythology, so essential to the Icelandic poet, was not suppressed in the interests of the new religion. In course of time the idea very naturally suggested itself that what had been done in Latin could also be done in Icelandic,—that a written literature was as possible in the one language as the other. The example of Old English may very well have had some share in awakening this idea, for it is quite certain that some of these early Icelandic scholars could read English manuscripts, the handwriting of which they imitated in several respects.

It was in the beginning of the twelfth century that the writing of Icelandic became an accomplished fact. "The first summer that Bergthór Hrafnsson was law-speaker (i.e. in 1117), it was decreed that our laws should be written in a book at the house of Hafliði Másson during the following winter, from the dictation of Bergthór and other learned men who were appointed for the purpose." The proposal was carried out, and the winter of 1117—18 thus became an eventful date for Icelandic literature, as it showed the way for putting down on parchment all that had hitherto lived in the memories and on the tongues of the Icelandic people.

The authority for this statement is a small work written within twelve or fifteen years later by one who may fairly be styled the father of Icelandic history. This was a western Icelander named Ari Thorgilsson, sometimes surnamed 'the priest' (*prestr*), and sometimes 'the learned' (*hinn fróði*); not seldom both epithets are combined. Ari was born in the year 1067, and his ancestry was sufficiently distinguished to encourage any natural tendency in his mind to a study of the past. On his father's side he was a descendant of Ólaf the White, who in the latter half of the ninth century was Norse king in Dublin. Ólaf's son, Thorstein the Red, made a league with Earl Sigurd of the Orkneys against the Scots; "they won Caithness and Sutherland, Ross and Moray, and more than half of Scotland. Thorstein was king over this, until the Scots played him false, and he fell there in battle." Thorstein's mother, a remarkable woman, left Scotland soon after this, and became one of the most famous among the early settlers in Iceland; from Thorstein's son, Ólaf Feilan, Ari was the sixth in descent. To trace his relationship to other men and women of note would be tedious, but it is worth mentioning that his great-grandfather, Thorkel, was one of the husbands of Guðrún, round whom the chief interest of *Laxdœla saga* centres, and that his mother's father had taken part in the battle of Clontarf. A knowledge of the careers and adventures of his own forefathers would in itself have been enough to establish Ari as an authority in biography and history.

At the age of seven, through the death of his father, Ari passed into the household of Hall Thórarinsson, who had his home in Haukadal in the southwest of Iceland. Hall was already a man of eighty, and had been settled in Haukadal for half a century, but in his younger days he had been an associate of Ólaf Haraldsson, that king of Norway who fell at Stiklastað in 1030, and came to be known as Ólaf the Saint. To Hall's great age, wide experience, and marvellous memory, Ari owed much of the historical knowledge he then acquired, either directly, or through another foster-son of Hall's, Teit, the son of Bishop Ísleif. As Ari himself says: "Teit was fostered by Hall in Haukadal, that man of whom it was universally said that he was the most generous and noble character to be found among the unschooled men of this country. I came to Hall when I was seven years old, and I was with him for fourteen winters." How far back Hall's recollections went is thus emphasized by Ari. "Hall told me so, and he was both truthful and had a good memory. He remembered his own baptism by Thangbrand, when he was three years old; that was the year before Christianity was adopted by law in this country."

Remarkably little is known of Ari's later life. He was one of those "men of rank who studied and were ordained as priests"; he was on terms of intimacy with the great men of his time, such as the bishops of Hólar and Skálholt, but even his place of abode is uncertain, though the probability is that he lived at Stað on Snæfellsness. The exact date of his death is known; it was Nov. 9, 1148.

Gifted with a genius for historical research, Ari seems to have devoted his life to collecting, comparing, and sifting the traditions and recollections of the most credible and capable men that he was able to come in contact with. The actual scope of his written work has been much discussed, and some points will probably always remain obscure, but the value of his researches in Icelandic and Scandinavian history is a fact as fully recognized by his own age as by modern scholars. Snorri Sturluson, in the prologue to his *Heimskringla*, bears eloquent testimony to the importance of his predecessor's work, and ends with the words: "It was no wonder though Ari was well informed with regard to historic events both here and abroad, for he had learned them from old and intelligent men, and was himself both eager to learn and had a good memory."

Ari's chief work was one entitled *Íslendinga-bók* or 'Book of Icelanders,' of which only a second and shorter recension, made by the author himself about 1130, has come down to us. This is a concise account of the settlement and early history of Iceland, in which special prominence is given to legal and ecclesiastical matters. Ari made special efforts to fix the exact date of every important event which he mentions, and his chronology was usually accepted as authoritative by later writers. He was also very careful to base his statements on the best authority available, and constantly gives the names of the persons on whom he relied for each particular piece of information. Thus he fixed the date of the settlement of Greenland from information given by his uncle Thorkel, and he again had it from a man who went there with Eirík the Red. Again, with reference to an incident connected with the introduction of Christianity into Iceland, he says: "Teit said that he learned this from one who was there."

This thoroughness in Ari's critical method made his work of great importance as a foundation for

Icelandic historical writing, and his services in this respect were probably far greater than appears even in the wonderful little booklet by which he is now represented. He was undoubtedly one of the great links between the saga-age (which ended about 1030) and the literary period (which began with his own work), though it is now impossible to judge how far he was the principal medium by which records of the past were preserved and transmitted to the next generation. The same uncertainty attaches to a slightly older contemporary, who holds a very prominent place in Icelandic tradition. Sæmund Sigfússon, also called 'the learned' and also a priest, living at Oddi in the south of Iceland, was born in 1056 and died in 1103. In early youth he had studied abroad, but returned to his native land in 1076. Sæmund had the same interest in historical studies as Ari, and is frequently cited as an authority on questions of fact and chronology, relating to the lives of the Norwegian kings. That he wrote some work on this subject appears to be certain, but it is extremely probable that it was in Latin, and was rather an outline of history than a detailed narrative.

The example set by Ari did not long remain unfruitful. During the second half of the twelfth century there must have been much literary activity in Iceland, and many pens must have been at work recording local and foreign history, whether handed down from earlier times by tradition, or learned by special inquiry from still living authorities. The names of some of these writers are known, and their works can be identified, but in the majority of cases they are writers who dealt specially with Norwegian history (see Chapter IV). Setting these aside for the present, there remains a still larger body of Icelandic literature which cannot be associated with the name of any writer whatsoever. This is the case with the whole series of sagas of famous Icelanders, with some sagas relating to neighbouring countries (as the Orkneys, Færöes, Denmark, etc.), and with all the sagas of a mythic or romantic character. How much material is comprehended in each of these classes will be more clearly understood after perusal of the chapters in which they are specially dealt with.

That such a mass of literature, much of it of great interest and high merit, should be to a great extent anonymous is very remarkable, considering how strong the force of tradition was in Iceland. It is true that in the middle ages there was a carelessness as to the exact authorship of literary works, to an extent that seems surprising at the present day, but nowhere does it appear to have been so prevalent as in Iceland. The explanation presumably lies in the fact that so much of the written matter had its origin in the oral narratives which had been transmitted in a set form for several generations. The first writers of these traditions probably did not add much of their own to the story as they had received it, and therefore saw no good grounds for claiming the title of authors. In other words, the ink and parchment were at first little more than a substitute for the human memory, and the skill of the teller or reader was still of more importance than the art of the writer. Another reason may be found in the way in which Icelandic writings were freely altered and adapted by any one who wished to copy them or utilise them for his own purposes. Icelanders of the thirteenth and fourteenth centuries were constantly abridging or expanding, combining or interpolating, re-arranging or re-writing, the works of their predecessors, and it would often have been impossible to assign the name of any single author to the form which they finally assumed. In some cases we know the names of the men who produced the existing recensions of a work, while that of the original writer has been completely lost.

It is clear, at any rate, that the authorship of the written saga was not usually regarded as a matter of great moment. Had it been so, the keen Icelandic interest in everything personal would assuredly have preserved the name of the writer along with his work. This is proved by the way in which the authorship of the old skaldic poems has been recorded in almost every instance. There would have been no greater difficulty in doing it in the case of the sagas, and the neglect of it indicates that some difference was felt. The poem was the actual production of the poet, and he alone had the sole credit of making it, whereas the saga was not in its origin the invention of the writer. This fact is of some importance towards deciding the question how far the older written sagas represent the earlier oral versions.

In the case of sagas which have a purely fictitious basis, the subject-matter gives but little clue to the date of their composition, or to the part of Iceland in which they were written. The sagas relating to Iceland itself reveal a little more on both of these heads, but not infrequently they also present features which render a precise answer impossible. As will be seen later, the sagas dealing with the older period—the saga-age proper—represent the west and north of Iceland in a far greater degree than they do the east and south; the proportion is actually something like ten to two. It is not difficult to infer from this that most of them were therefore written in the west and north, seeing that so much in the stories themselves has a strong local interest, and would naturally be most fully preserved in the district, and in the families, to which the leading persons belonged. A close examination of a saga often confirms this, to the extent of absolute certainty. The unknown author may plainly indicate not only his district, but even his own part of that district, either by a minute knowledge of the locality, or by the adverbs of direction which he employs. It is often easy to perceive that outside of a certain area his knowledge of places, and of their relative positions and distances from each other, is vague, while within that area he is familiar with every foot of the ground. The same local knowledge is often displayed in the genealogies which occur in most of the sagas; the author is well informed in the history and relationships of certain families, while as to others his knowledge is limited or inaccurate. In some cases it is not difficult to conjecture to which family he himself belonged.

These frequent genealogies are among the most useful indications which the sagas give as to the date of their composition; but in using them for this purpose some caution is necessary, as nothing was more likely to be inserted by the copier of a saga than a later name in the family tree. The relative dates of different sagas may also sometimes be inferred from the fact that one cites another as its authority for a special piece of information, or as giving a fuller account of some episode. Here, however, there are two complications to be considered. It is not always certain whether the references are to a written saga, or to the current oral version; and such citations might very easily be inserted by later copyists. Hence the most diverse views as to the date of a saga have sometimes been based on the very same passages, some scholars holding them to be mere interpolations in an early text, while others contend that they are integral parts of the narrative and prove that it is late.

To some extent, also, the date of a saga may be inferred from its style, and from its manner of telling the story. The simpler and purer the style, and the more straightforward the narrative, the earlier it is likely to be; a more elaborate diction, and tendency to a romantic tone and colouring, are indications of a period when the influence of foreign romances had begun to be felt. Again, however, there is the difficulty of deciding whether the text in the latter case is the original one, or has been worked over by a later hand, in order to bring it more into accordance with the prevailing taste. In some cases it is quite obvious that this has happened, for both the earlier and later versions of the saga are preserved, in whole or in part, and thus the process of conversion to the more romantic and less thoroughly national form can be clearly traced.

The problems which attend the serious study of the older Icelandic literature are thus many and complicated, and it is only by slow degrees that the general outlines of the subject have been clearly made out. Many questions still remain obscure, and it is possible that a number of them can never be satisfactorily answered, through the lack of early material to help in the investigation. Although it is fairly clear that the written saga took its rise about the middle of the twelfth century, and that its most flourishing period was between that date and the end of the thirteenth (i.e. from about 1150 to 1300), very few saga-texts from that time have been preserved. Early Icelandic manuscripts, dating from about 1200 onwards, chiefly contain religious or ecclesiastical works; those of the historical, traditional, and legendary sagas mainly belong to the fourteenth and fifteenth centuries. In not a few instances, indeed, the text survives only in paper copies made in the seventeenth, or even in the eighteenth, century. During the sixteenth and seventeenth centuries there was considerable destruction of older manuscripts, and it is quite certain that much valuable matter has thus been lost. The destruction would probably have been still greater, had not the Icelandic language undergone so little change during the centuries; the fact that even very old manuscripts were still perfectly intelligible to any one who cared to read them must have greatly assisted towards their preservation. Even at the present day, Iceland has a great advantage over most European countries, in being able with perfect ease to read and understand its best mediæval literature. It is possible in Iceland to publish popular editions of the sagas, without any modernizing of the language, and within recent years such editions have been extensively printed and read. During the nineteenth century the study of the older literature has had a great influence upon the style of the best Icelandic prose, which is now purer and more flexible than it has been at any time since the fourteenth century. The genuine type of saga-prose is a purely natural style, developed from the form in which the stories were originally told; it is in fact almost the only prose style of Western Europe which has had a perfectly natural and independent development. The result is that it is extremely hard to reproduce it successfully in any other language.

Although the contents of the different classes of sagas are fully explained in the following chapters, some general indication may be given here of their value as historical records. In the first place, as already said, they are by far the fullest authorities for the details of early Scandinavian history, and they throw much light upon the history of the British Islands during several centuries. Moreover, they give most of this historical information in no dry annalistic manner, but in a form that is replete with life and colour. They bring before the reader, almost as in a picture, those Scandinavian leaders who played such an important part in Western Europe, and altered the whole fortunes of countries like England and France. They do not merely record the names and exploits of these men: they present the very men themselves, their character, their aims, their daily life and occupations. It is the great triumph of the saga-writers that they have succeeded in giving an almost complete picture of old Scandinavian life in all its aspects, and thus help towards an understanding of the early civilization of the other Germanic races. They are also masters in the delineation of character, sometimes by a brief indication of the leading qualities in the man or woman spoken of, but much more often by the mere action of the story itself. Among the hundreds of real persons who crowd the pages of the Icelandic sagas, it is surprising how many can be clearly and sharply distinguished from each other, and how skilfully the writers have brought out the contrasts between them. There are scores of Icelandic men and women, of all ranks in life, whose history and characters are so clearly presented in the sagas, that far more is known of them than of most of the kings of Britain at the same date.

In addition to their historical matter, the sagas have preserved an immense mass of information relating to old beliefs and customs, some of which must at one time have been widely spread among the Germanic peoples. While the old poetry, and Snorri Sturluson's *Edda*, contain practically all that is known about old Scandinavian mythology, the sagas give nearly all the information relative to the old religion;

and outside of that, all that is known of early Germanic religion is meagre indeed. In the beliefs which lie on the borders of mythology and religion, in the supernatural of every kind, the sagas are extremely rich, and few literatures possess more impressive ghost-stories. On this account the sagas are of immense value to the student of folk-lore, even if great caution must be exercised in drawing inferences from them, for reasons which will appear in a subsequent chapter.

CHAPTER III

HISTORICAL SAGAS RELATING TO ICELAND AND GREENLAND

The contents of Ari's *Islendinga-bók*, and of *Landnáma-bók*, would be sufficient in themselves to show that a very great knowledge of the past history of the island existed in Iceland in the twelfth century; but it would have been impossible to imagine how rich and full the traditions actually were, if so many of them had not formed the bases of separate sagas. In almost every district of Iceland, but especially (as we have already said) in the west and north, the memory of great men and distinguished families had been handed down, and out of these traditions came the collection of sagas now commonly grouped under the name of *Islendinga sögur*. Although they may thus be classed under a common title, and have certain characteristic features in common, these sagas differ greatly from each other in length, and in the extent to which they can be regarded as having a genuinely historical character. Some are quite short, covering thirty or forty small pages, or even less, while the larger extend to two, three, or even four hundred. In most cases it is clear that the shorter sagas are more original, or represent an earlier literary stage, than the longer ones; the latter are either composite, made up by working together two or three separate narratives, or belong to a period when the art of literary composition was more advanced. If only the more authentic sagas relating to events prior to 1030 are reckoned, their total number amounts to about 30, which in all would fill more than 3000 pages similar to those in this book. The geographical distribution of these is very unequal. The five longer sagas, which would occupy about 1400 pages, relate to the western half of Iceland; and of the remainder at least seven-eighths are connected with the west and north, the east and south-east being represented by a mere handful of very short stories.

In by far the greater number of these sagas the main action takes place at some period between the middle of the tenth century and the first quarter of the eleventh. In many of them, however, the story begins at an earlier date; not uncommonly some account is given of the ancestors of the hero, whether in Iceland itself or before the emigration to that island. Occasionally this part is so fully treated that the proper subject of the saga is quite late in making its appearance; in such cases there is often much valuable information relating to the times immediately before and after the settlement. The value, however, depends on the character of the saga, and it is often a doubtful question how far the accounts are derived from genuine tradition, and how much is due to historical studies in the thirteenth century. Even the genealogies of the settlers, which are sometimes given with great fulness, cannot be regarded as perfectly reliable for more than one or two generations previous to the settlement.

In giving some account of the extensive body of saga-literature relating directly to Iceland, or to its colony, Greenland, it will be best to divide it into four classes or groups, which to a great extent correspond to the historical development of the saga. The first two classes comprise the shorter and longer sagas of famous Icelanders, or of Icelandic families, during the older period, which closes about 1030. The third class consists of the sagas relating to the introduction of Christianity and the subsequent history of the Church in Iceland; these cover an otherwise barren century, and then from about 1120 run parallel to, or are closely connected with, an increasing volume of more secular history which reaches its latest point shortly after 1260.

It is obviously impossible, in the compass of an outline like this, to enter into details of all the separate sagas coming under these different heads. At the same time, it is only by giving some account, however much condensed, of a considerable number of them that their great variety and interest can be clearly displayed. In the following pages, therefore, the majority of them are named and described more or less fully, although with omission of many matters which a closer study of them would necessarily involve.

§ i. *The Shorter Sagas.* The best and most interesting of these amount to about a score in all, and contain a surprising variety of incident, whether genuine or fictitious, and much skilful delineation of personal character. Some of them are masterpieces of story-telling, but their full merit cannot always be appreciated unless they are read in the original language, and with a knowledge of the local conditions. The author, being as a rule well acquainted with the scene of the saga and perfectly familiar with the relationship of the persons concerned in it, is apt to assume the same knowledge on the part of his readers; for this reason it is often necessary to make a close study of the geography of the district and of several genealogies, before the whole course of the story becomes quite clear.

Of the short self-contained stories which probably represent most closely the primitive type of saga, one of the best is *Hrafnkels saga*, the action of which takes place in the east of Iceland (and at the Althingi), about the middle of the tenth century. The story, written by someone with thorough local knowledge and an interest in the past history of the district, is excellently told, and forms a neatly rounded tale, with an unexpected turn at the close. The whole series of events arises in a natural way out of Hrafnkel's personal character, coupled with his possession of a horse, which he had dedicated to the god Frey, and with regard to which he had made a rash vow. The fulfilment of this, almost against his own will, brought on his temporary downfall, and destroyed all his faith in the god, whose priest he had previously been. Both Hrafnkel's own case, and that of his chief adversary, are striking examples of the pride that goes before a fall—a sentiment which the saga itself expresses in a proverb. The serious character of the story is cleverly relieved by scenes of a lighter character at the Althingi, where a chief's festered toe was humorously utilized as a means of enlisting his sympathy on the side of the injured, and thus enabling those whom Hrafnkel had despised to triumph over him. Their subsequent want of foresight enabled Hrafnkel to requite them in full and recover his old position, with his character greatly improved by the reverse of fortune he had thus experienced. The delineation of character in this saga is remarkably good, and there is a striking air of impartiality and quiet forbearance about it, suggestive of a peace-loving honest-minded writer.

Another saga of the east of Iceland, and relating to events of much the same date as those in Hrafnkel's saga, is the short story of Thorstein the White, which contains some typical incidents. One of these forms the mainspring of the action. Thorstein the Fair, after his betrothal to Helga, decided to go abroad before settling down. Illness detained him in Norway, but his comrade Einar returned to Iceland, spread a report of his death, and succeeded in winning Helga for himself. As Thorstein recovered, it was a matter of course that he should subsequently avenge himself on his false associate, and almost inevitable that other innocent persons should be drawn into the blood-feud and lose their lives. Among these was Thorgils, son of Thorstein the White, on whom the loss fell all the more hardly, as he had the misfortune of being blind. Five years later Thorstein the Fair came back to Iceland, and immediately rode to the house of his namesake, not in order to revive the old quarrel, but with an offer to settle it by full payment for the death of Thorgils. "Thorstein the White said that he would not carry his son in his purse. Thorstein the Fair then springs up, and lays his head on the knee of his namesake." This absolute submission touched the blind father's heart, and he not only forgave everything, but insisted that Thorstein should stay with him and take charge of his household. The further relations between the two afford a fine example of the magnanimity which, in many of the sagas, stands in strong contrast to the implacable spirit of the ordinary blood-feud. There is a very similar transition from hostility to friendship at the end of *Vápnfirðinga saga*, which relates to the same district and partly to the same family; the events take place between 980 and 990. It is mainly a record of local dissensions, arising in the first instance out of covetousness, and here the generous character of Thorleif the Christian comes out in clear relief against the self-interest of the other chief actors. This saga is much longer than that of Thorstein, but both of them appear to be honest reproductions of local tradition, without any attempt at invention or the introduction of extraneous matter.

Still another saga from the same quarter of the island appears to rest on a good family tradition, the great-grandson of one of the leading persons being specially mentioned as the authority for it. This is the story of Helgi and Grím, the two sons of a widow named Droplaug, who at the ages of 13 and 12 avenge a reflection upon their mother's character by killing the author of the slander. This youthfulness of the heroes is a common feature in many sagas, and it is difficult to say how far it is merely conventional. Through this and other acts the two came into conflict with the leading man of the district, Helgi Ásbjarnarson; the older brother, Helgi, was the chief cause of these troubles, the younger being of a quiet and inoffensive disposition. Helgi's doings finally led to his being sentenced to banishment for three years; but like some more famous outlaws he chose to run the risks of remaining in Iceland, exposed at any moment to the lawful attack of his enemies. What the end would be was darkly shown to him by forebodings and dreams, such as are prominent in many of the sagas, and which no doubt had a foundation in real experience. At last his foes found their opportunity, and after a gallant fight (the description of which is one of the best parts of the saga) Helgi was killed and Grím severely wounded. The latter recovered, but "he never laughed after the death of Helgi." The story of how he avenged his brother by entering his enemy's house at night is a striking one, and is well told. Subsequently, though with some difficulty, he succeeded in getting away from Iceland and arrived in Norway; there he was reported to have died from wounds received in a duel with a viking, who had arrogantly demanded in marriage the sister of his Norwegian host. There is a conventional touch in this which renders its authenticity doubtful, but the story as a whole has an air of truth about it; some of the incidents are corroborated by verses, most of them composed by Grím himself. The events belong to the later part of the saga-age, from about 980 to 1006; and Grím's great-grandson, who 'told the saga' might well have lived a good way into the twelfth century.

Various sagas relating to the north of Iceland also appear to be, in the main, good representatives of a genuine tradition. Several of these belong to the district round about Eyjafirth, in the eastern half of the north coast, and contain much interesting matter; some particulars relating to these it may be useful to mention briefly, a full account of each saga being out of the question. For the most part these sagas relate to events which took place between 970 and 1030; but one begins much earlier, and another ends with incidents of a generation later. Two are named after the hero of the story: these are the sagas of Víga-Glúm and Valla-Ljót. Another two have more comprehensive titles, and are called the sagas of the men of Reykjadal (*Reykdœla saga*) and of Ljósavatn (*Ljósvetninga saga*). That of Valla-Ljót is the shortest, and Ljósvetninga the longest, of the four. The former has but slight literary value

and is not of special interest; it is mainly an account
of a conflict between Ljót and another chief, Guðmund
the Mighty, which was soon ended by mutual agreement (in 1010). The saga of Víga-Glúm is in every
way superior to this, and contains much interesting
information as to old customs and beliefs. Glúm
began his energetic career at an early age, and the
story of his later life covers a period of some fifty
years, down to his death in 1003. This is one of the
few sagas which throw some real light upon the old
religion of Iceland, as it not only makes mention of
Frey's temple in Eyjafirth, but has preserved some
ideas relating to the god himself and his attitude
towards his worshippers. The disputes for the
possession of a certain field bring into prominence
the fact that for some centuries after the settlement
there was a considerable amount of agriculture
in Iceland; traces of this still appear largely in
local names throughout the island. The old sport
of horse-fighting and the pastime of 'choosing confidants' have also a part in the sequence of events.
A curious incident is that of Glúm's oath, in which
by the ambiguous use of a word he seemed to clear
himself from a charge of manslaughter; the record of
the procedure and the formula employed are of considerable value for Icelandic legal antiquities. All
Glúm's fighting brought him little profit in the end;
he was driven from his homestead, became old and

blind, and died immediately after having accepted the new faith which had come to Iceland.

Glúm also enters to some extent into the second portion of *Reykdœla saga*, the hero of which is Víga-Skúta; in the earlier portion the leading persons are Skúta's father, Áskel, and the latter's nephew Vémund. The action takes place in the second half of the tenth century, and the author has evidently done his best to give the story as he found it in the district. The longer *Ljósvetninga saga*, also based on a good tradition, is composed of several sections which have only a loose connexion with each other. The central portion relates to the famous chief Guðmund the Mighty, and ends with his sudden death in 1025. The remainder of the saga relates to Guðmund's sons, Eyjólf and Koðrán, and deals with events which took place as late as between 1050 and 1065, a period lying altogether outside of that which constitutes the 'saga-age' proper.

A different and less original type of saga is represented by one from a district further west than the preceding—the story of the men of Vatnsdal (*Vatnsdœla saga*), in which the fortunes of a family for nearly two hundred years are told. The narrative here begins very early, with distinguished Norwegians belonging to the first half of the ninth century; how much of this is genuine tradition is very doubtful. There can be no question, however, of the historical existence of Ingimund, who was a viking and fought for King Harald at Hafrsfirth in 872. He refused to believe the prophecy of a Finnish wise-woman, who told him that he was destined to end his days in Iceland; but fate proved too strong for him, and in the end everything went as she had foretold. The power of fate is in fact the connecting thread which runs all through the saga, and occasionally finds expression in proverbial sayings. After the death of Ingimund, and the avenging of him, the connexion between the various parts of the saga becomes much looser, so that the latter half is less interesting and attractive than the earlier. In the saga as a whole there is much information about old beliefs, old religious rites, and early customs, all narrated in a style which shows considerable literary training as well as a marked interest in history and antiquities. A different version of some of the incidents is given in *Finnboga saga,* and a comparison of the two accounts is instructive as to the difference between the historical and the fictitious element in the Icelandic sagas.

In four or five of the shorter sagas the hero is a poet (a *skáld*), and in all of these there is more or less of a love-element present. As revealed in these sagas, the poets are striking and interesting characters —impulsive, self-willed men, as ready with the sword as with the tongue, and usually the authors of their own misfortunes. The best known of these stories are those of Kormák and Gunnlaug, the latter of which has attracted much attention, and has been frequently translated into other languages. Kormák is the earliest of the poets thus commemorated, but the relation of his saga to fact is far from certain. His active career was a brief one (from about 956 to 967), and part of that time he spent in Norway and Ireland. As a poet he is known from other sources, and in the saga nearly seventy verses are cited as his; the majority of these may be genuine, but many of them are in a very corrupt state. The saga is mainly concerned with his relations to Steingerð; many of the verses refer to her, and some of them hold the foremost place in old Icelandic love-poetry. Kormák did not marry Steingerð—through witchcraft, it is suggested—and she was given in marriage to Bersi, also a poet and a good fighter. With him, and with her second husband, Kormák fought duels, and continued to be influenced by his love for her, until he met with an early death during a viking raid in Scotland. The incidents in the saga hang somewhat loosely together, and are not told in the clearest fashion, nor is the prose always in agreement with the verses. Part of the narrative may have been taken from a separate saga of Bersi, a number of whose verses are also cited. There are several interesting passages, such as that which describes the first meeting of Kormák and Steingerð, the borrowing of the sword Sköfnung, the old regulations concerning duels, and the means by which one witch-wife endeavoured to counteract the spells imposed by another.

The saga of Gunnlaug is much shorter, and its literary merit much higher, than that of Kormák. He was in love with Helga the Fair, the daughter of Thorstein at Borg ; but during his prolonged absence from Iceland (from 1001 to 1005) she was married to Hrafn, whom Gunnlaug had provoked by his contemptuous behaviour while they were together at the court of the Swedish king. The enmity between them led to an indecisive duel at the Althingi, and was ended by another in Norway (in 1008), in which both of the combatants were killed. There are many striking passages and incidents in the saga, such as the dream of Thorstein, in which the whole course of events is foreshadowed ; the story of Helga's birth and upbringing ; Gunnlaug's travels abroad, in the course of which he visited not only Norway and Sweden, but England, Ireland, and the Orkneys as well ; the rivalry of the two poets at the Swedish court, and their criticisms of each other's poetry ; the last fight on Dinganess, and the touching death of Helga, with Gunnlaug's gift before her eyes. It is undoubtedly the love-story running through it that has drawn so much attention to this saga, but the prominence of this element has awakened some doubt as to the perfect genuineness of the tale. There are some indications that in tone it may have been influenced by a knowledge of foreign romances, although its historical basis need not be doubted. Gunnlaug's visits to England and Ireland are sufficiently attested by the fragments of his poems in praise of King Ethelred and Earl Sigtrygg; of the other verses contained in the saga some are certainly spurious, but a few may well be genuine.

The saga of Hallfreð 'the troublesome poet' (*vandræðaskáld*) has some resemblance to that of Kormák, with Kolfinna in the place of Steingerð; it is, however, much shorter and of a more historical character. The most valuable parts of the saga are not those which deal with the love-affair, but those which tell of Hallfreð's visits to Norway and his coming in contact with King Ólaf Tryggvason. The king induced him to become a Christian, but this he did only upon certain conditions, and even threatened to relapse when the king refused to listen to his verses. "I will give up the lore that you have made me learn," he said, "if you will not listen to my poem; for what you have made them teach me is not more poetic than the poem I have composed about you." Several of his verses show the reluctance with which he gave up the old faith, and supply important evidence as to the hold which the worship of Odin and the other gods had upon the Scandinavian mind. There is also an account of an expedition to Sweden, where he married and settled down for two or three years. Hallfreð ran many risks in the course of his adventurous life, and was only forty years old when he died at sea, as the result of an accident, in 1007. His coffin drifted to Iona, and his body was finally buried in the church there. In certain respects Hallfreð was a greater poet than either Kormák or Gunnlaug, but his love-verses are few and of little note in comparison with his other work; finest of all is his memorial poem for Ólaf Tryggvason, in whose last battle it was not his fortune to take a part.

The story of the two poets Björn and Thórð, told in *Bjarnar saga Hítdœlakappa*, has some resemblance to that of Gunnlaug and Hrafn, but in this case the two rivals came much more into contact with each other. Björn was engaged to Oddný, but went abroad (in 1007), and like Gunnlaug stayed too long; his absence gave Thórð the chance of stepping in before him and securing the bride for himself. This was a distinct breach of faith on the part of Thórð, between whom and Björn there had been a grudge, followed by apparent friendship. The subsequent relations between the two rivals were peculiar, sometimes at enmity, sometimes nominally reconciled; for a time Björn even stayed in Thórð's house. Satirical verses composed by each against the other increased the growing bitterness between them, and at last the breach became final. Thórð then (in 1024) lay in wait for Björn with a strong body of men, and killed him after a prolonged and gallant resistance. Björn's death told so much upon Oddný that after it she gradually pined away, and the saga sketches very touchingly the unavailing regret of Thórð, who "would rather have had Björn alive again" than witness the sufferings of his wife.—Björn's adventures in other lands, some of them undoubtedly fictitious, are pretty fully narrated in the saga, which also cites a number of verses by each of the poets. Thórð is otherwise known as a skald, and Björn is said to have composed a poem in praise of the apostle Thomas, to whom he built a church in Iceland. "So said Rúnólf Dálksson," an Icelandic priest in the middle of the twelfth century; this reference would indicate an early date for the saga, but it has scarcely come down in its original form.

There is also a slight love-interest in the story of the poet Thormóð Bersason, commonly called *kolbrúnarskáld*, from the verses which he composed in praise of Thorbjörg, surnamed *kolbrún* on account of her coal-black eyebrows. These verses he afterwards adapted to suit a new love, but Thorbjörg appeared to him in a dream, reproached him with his unfaithfulness, and afflicted him with a pain in the eyes, which proved so violent that he was fain to be freed from it by making an open confession of his fault. The greater part of this saga, however, is concerned with matters of a different kind. At an early age Thormóð had entered into sworn brotherhood with Thorgeir Hávarsson, and they had vowed that the longer lived of the two should avenge the other. From this close association between them, their story has received the inexact title of the 'saga of the foster-brothers' (*Fóstbrœðra saga*). Thorgeir, who was a man of great strength and rough disposition, was finally killed in the north-east of Iceland (in 1024) by a certain Thorgrím from Greenland. Thormóð, though he had long before parted company from his friend, felt himself bound by his oath to avenge him, and went to Greenland for the purpose. His adventures there, especially after he had killed Thorgrím, are very fully related, and form one of the most exciting sections of the saga; their authenticity is to a great extent vouched for by the exactness of the local geography. In the end he was able to escape from Greenland, and returned to Norway; there he attached himself to King Ólaf Haraldsson, and accompanied him in his subsequent exile. When Ólaf made the vain attempt to recover his kingdom in 1030, Thormóð went with him, and on the morning of the battle at Stiklastað woke up the king's host by his recitation of the old war-poem *Bjarkamál*. That day he fought desperately, and was not wounded till the very close of the battle, when an arrow pierced his breast. The account of what followed on this, until he fell dead with an unfinished verse upon his tongue, is one of the most striking passages in old Icelandic literature. Altogether the saga is a notable piece of work, though in its present form it bears the marks of a late hand, which has here and there inserted passages displaying an inflated style and wanting in good taste. Thormóð was of considerable note as a poet, and some forty of his verses are preserved, fifteen of them being from a poem commemorative of his comrade Thorgeir.

The saga of Gísli Súrsson (*Gísla saga*) is also that of a poet, and no mean one, but its hero is still more famous as one of the great Icelandic outlaws, who chose rather to face privations and death than give way to their enemies by leaving the country. Gísli was a Norwegian by birth, and went to Iceland with his father about 935, after revenging wrongs done to them in their native land. They settled in Dýrafirth, in the north-west of the island, and soon contracted relationships with some of the earlier settlers. After some years, Gísli's sworn brother Véstein was murdered by Thorgrím, a local chief who had married Gísli's sister. In pursuance of his duty to his dead kinsman, Gísli then killed Thorgrím, but in such a way that the author of the deed remained unknown for a time, and the secret was only disclosed by his own imprudence. Gísli was subsequently outlawed (in 965), and lived in that condition for thirteen years. The whole story of his outlawry, his hairbreadth escapes and steadily increasing hardships, is very touchingly related, and is rendered still more impressive by his ill-boding dreams; in these he constantly saw one or other of two 'dream-women,' one of them well-disposed to him, the other the reverse. As time went on, the former appeared more and more seldom, and at last his dreams affected him so much that he was afraid to remain alone in his hiding-places. During all his troubles he received the faithful aid of his wife, Auð, whose devotion to her husband is the bright thread running through the saga. In the end Gísli fell before his enemies, after a defence as stubborn as that of Björn; "and it is commonly said that he was a most brave and gallant man, though not in all things a fortunate one."

Among the minor sagas worth mentioning, there are several which in different ways present a story obviously diverging from the sphere of fact into that of fiction. One of these is the saga of Gold-Thórir (*Gullþóris saga*) or of the men of Thorskafirth (*Þorskfirðinga saga*). In its original form this was evidently a sober unadorned record of dissension and fighting between local chiefs within a very limited area, every foot of which was familiar to the writer of the saga. As it now exists, the true beginning has disappeared, and its place has been taken by a purely fanciful account of Thórir's adventures in Norway; in this the conventional method of obtaining treasure by digging into a grave-mound is slightly varied, as the buried berserk prevents Thórir from carrying out his design, and directs him to a greater source of wealth. To obtain this, Thórir and his comrades had to enter, at great risk, a cave inhabited by dragons, and were rewarded for their daring by abundance of gold, from which Thórir derived his later distinctive epithet. In the more genuine portions, which describe events taking place round the inner end of Broadfirth between the years 920 and 940, there is very little plot; the author evidently had tried to do no more than piece together the local traditions in their proper sequence, and more than once explains the grounds on which certain statements are made. Here and there, as in so many sagas, a belief in the supernatural powers of certain persons makes its appearance, and it is quite impossible to say at what period in the development of the story these features were introduced. Their conventional nature is sufficiently clear from the frequency of their occurrence in saga-literature.

The deviation from fact is of quite a different character in the saga of Hœnsa-Thórir, which contains nothing of an improbable nature. It is a tale of a mean man—one who had traded in fowls and was on that account called Hen-Thórir—and a man of note, Blund-Ketil, whose desire to help others led to his own undoing. During a hard winter he took hay from Thórir in order to give it to others who required it, and on account of this Thórir never rested until he had drawn some of the most powerful men in the district to burn Blund-Ketil in his house by night. The rest of the saga tells how this deed was avenged by Blund-Ketil's son, and how at last peace was made between the opposing parties. The delineation of character in the story is remarkably good, and some of the incidents are vividly described. In spite of its air of veracity, however, there are strong reasons for regarding it as mainly a product of literary invention; one of the strongest is the fact, which has Ari's authority behind it, that it was not Blund-Ketil but his son Thorkel who was burned by his enemies (in 965).

Of a somewhat similar type, as regards its correspondence with real facts, is the saga of Hávarð the Lame, who was a real person and a poet. The general outline of the story may well be historic; but there is much confusion, and probably a good deal of invention, in the details. It tells how Ólaf, the son of Hávarð, was wantonly killed by a prominent man in Ísafirth, about the year 1000, and how the aged father, against all expectation, carried out the difficult task of avenging him. After this he left his own district, and moved a far way to the east, to Svarfaðardal. Here the story was evidently handed down, and finally written by some one who had no exact knowledge of the locality in which the action took place.

The history of Svarfaðardal itself during the greater part of the tenth century forms the subject of *Svarfdœla saga*, which must also be regarded as largely fictitious. Several of the conventional incidents are represented in it, such as fighting with vikings and berserks; and one of the chief persons, Klaufi, takes an active part in affairs after he is dead. One of the most striking characters in the saga is a woman, Yngvild of the fair cheeks, whose share in bringing about the death of Klaufi was relentlessly punished by his kinsman Karl the Red. The treatment by which he finally succeeded in breaking her proud spirit is fortunately not typical of the saga-age, and may well be invention from beginning to end. There was evidently an older saga relating to the same district, but how much of it remains in the existing one it is impossible to determine.

Another case in which a late fictitious version has replaced an earlier and more genuine narrative is the saga of the two foster-brothers Hörð and Geir, who finally became the leaders of a band of outlaws and robbers living on an island in Hvalfirth. Previous to this they had been abroad, and are credited with battles against vikings, breaking into grave-mounds, laying ghosts, and other stock adventures. In the end the band became too troublesome for the neighbouring district, and were decoyed to land and killed there (about 986). Though it possesses little or no historical value, *Harðar saga* has considerable literary merit, and even invests the fate of the outlaws with a certain tragic pathos.

Among the shorter sagas there are several which deal more or less with Greenland, one of which (*Fóstbrœðra saga*) has already been mentioned. The discovery and settlement of that country are briefly related in the opening chapters of the saga of Eirík the Red (also, and with more reason, called the saga of Thorfinn Karlsefni). Some events in the early history of the settlement are then recounted, and here occurs the fullest extant description of an old Icelandic 'spae-wife' and her methods of divination. There are also strange tales of hauntings and dead men's prophecies, mingled with matter of great historical and geographical interest. Leif, the son of Eirík, had been in Norway and had there accepted the Christian faith. On his way back to Greenland he was driven out of his course, and came to a strange land, which either then or soon afterwards received the name of Vínland. Some years later (apparently in 1007) an expedition sailed in search of Vínland, under the leadership of Thorfinn, and the later part of the saga gives an account of its fortunes. The details given in this account have been much discussed and disputed, and the matter is complicated by the existence of a very different form of the story, but there is no reason to doubt the general fact that Thorfinn and his comrades explored a considerable part of the eastern coast of North America. Vínland and its inhabitants are alluded to by Ari Thorgilsson, obviously as something well known, and Ari's information came from very reliable sources. Moreover, Thorfinn's son Snorri, who was born in Vínland, was the immediate ancestor of several famous Icelandic bishops, and it is in the highest degree improbable that these would have been mistaken in matters so closely connected with their family history.

There is a good deal about Greenland in *Flóamanna saga*, which tells how Thorgils from Flói, in the south-west of Iceland, went out there on the invitation of Eirík the Red, and suffered many hardships both on the voyage and in the country itself. The story of these is very well told, but their authenticity is extremely doubtful. The adventures of Thormóð appear to have a much better foundation; and a genuine glimpse of life in Greenland in the twelfth century is afforded by a short story preserved in the great Flatey-book.

The works of which some account has been given in the preceding pages do not quite exhaust the list of the shorter sagas, but those which remain do not present any features of an essentially different nature. One, however, deserves mention for two reasons. It is of a lighter type than the others, being more of a comedy than a tragedy, and it deals with a later period than any other (except the latter portion of *Ljósvetninga*), as the events related in it took place about the middle of the eleventh century. This is *Bandamanna saga*, the 'story of the confederates,' and its theme is how six or seven influential chiefs were befooled and rendered ridiculous by the craft of one old man, who in this way rendered an important service to his son. The saga is interesting not only for its unusual subject, but for the glimpse it gives of life in Iceland during this comparatively peaceful period of its history. To the same century, however, belong the greater number of the short stories of Icelanders, which are not found as separate compositions, but are interwoven in the longer versions of the sagas of Norwegian kings and are known by the name of *thættir* (in the singular *tháttr*, a word properly meaning a strand of a cord or rope). Many of these are of great merit and interest, and bring out very clearly the prominent part which Icelanders continued to play in Norway and other countries during this period.

§ ii. *The Longer Sagas.* Five of the sagas relating to early Iceland stand out from the others by reason of their greater length, though the shortest of them is not so much longer than one or two of those already mentioned. In addition to their length, they are also characterized by their excellence, and are commonly recognized as reaching the highest levels of Icelandic literary art. In several respects, however, they differ very clearly from each other, and their historical value is by no means the same. The most reliable in this way is the shortest of the five, which bears the inappropriate name of *Eyrbyggja saga*, and is especially valuable for the information it has preserved relative to the old Scandinavian religious beliefs and practices. It is the story of events which took place on the great peninsula of Snæfellsness, on the west coast of Iceland, between the period of the settlement (about 884) and the death of the famous chief Snorri (about 1031). The early chapters tell how Thórólf from Mostr in Norway went out to Iceland, taking with him the timber of Thór's temple, which he re-erected at the place where he made his new home. The whole passage relating to this contains much of all that is known about the actual worship of Thór among the old Norwegians and Icelanders, and appears to rest upon a trustworthy tradition. With the exception of a few events of slight importance, the saga then passes rapidly over more than half a century from the death of Thórólf, and the main narrative begins (about 978) with the rise of the young Snorri, a son of that Thorgrím for whose death Gísli was outlawed.

Snorri took up his abode at Helgafell, the hill which Thórólf had regarded as sacred, and is one of the principal figures throughout the rest of the saga. For a time he had a strong rival in Arnkel, a near neighbour, but the contest between them ended in the fall of the latter (about 993). Some fifteen years later Snorri exchanged homesteads with the famous Guðrún (see p. 64), and so left the neighbourhood; nor does the saga have much to tell about his later doings, although he lived for twenty years after this. In the saga as a whole there is much dissension and fighting, and one of these encounters was the occasion of a good deal of verse-making by a certain Thórarinn. There are also stories of berserks and sorcery and hauntings; in respect of the latter this saga is especially powerful, and the account of the Hebridean woman Thorgunna, her death, and the subsequent marvels at Fróðá, forms one of the most striking passages of the kind in old Icelandic literature. Although *Eyrbyggja* is less of a connected story than many of the other sagas, the separate portions of it are interesting and well written. The author clearly belonged to the district, was well acquainted with its traditions and poetry, and had a sound historical sense in spite of his delight in the marvellous. Apart from the sections in which this interest predominates, there is no reason to doubt the substantial accuracy of the narrative.

Of a different type is the much longer *Egils saga*, to which a very prominent place must be assigned, not only on account of its length and the variety of its incidents, but also for its masterly arrangement and lucid style. It also begins at an early date, with men who were grown up before Harald the Fair-haired began to extend his rule over the whole of Norway. Two of these, Kveldúlf and his son Skallagrím, finally took revenge upon Harald for the death of another son, Thórólf, and thereupon set sail for Iceland. Kveldúlf died at sea, but Skallagrím reached his destination, took possession of a large district on the west coast, and made his homestead at Borg in Mýrar. The account of all this, together with some other matters, takes up about one-third of the saga; the rest of it relates entirely to Egil, the son of Skallagrím, and gives a full account both of his adventures abroad and his doings in Iceland itself down to his death in 982. These adventures are too varied for enumeration here ; prominent among them are his visits to England, where he fought for King Athelstan against the Scots and their allies, and on a later occasion saved his head at York by composing, in the course of one night, a poem in praise of his enemy, Earl Eirík. Two other poems by Egil are given in the saga, one in praise of his trusty friend Arinbjörn, and the other on the loss of his sons. One of these had died, another was drowned in

Borgarfirth, and Egil was with difficulty prevented from starving himself to death. At the request of his daughter he composed the poem, in which resignation and resentment are curiously blended and powerfully expressed. Many single verses are also cited throughout the saga as being by Egil, but it is not quite clear how many of these are authentic. It is even uncertain how far the saga as a whole can be regarded as historical; much in it was no doubt drawn from local tradition, but the writer was clearly a man capable of handling his materials in a very independent manner, and there is every likelihood that he did so. The view has been advanced that the saga may actually be the work of Snorri Sturluson, who lived at Borg from 1201 to 1206; both the style and the historical knowledge, so apparent in every part of it, are strongly in favour of this attribution, though it can scarcely be regarded as proved. In any case the author was some one with thorough local knowledge, who took a deep interest in all that related to his hero and the family to which he belonged. In spite of its containing the history of three generations, the saga is so skilfully put together that the interest goes on by a natural sequence from the beginning to the end, and forms a very fine specimen of Icelandic literary skill.

Another of the longer sagas, that of the Laxdale men (*Laxdœla saga*), also gives the story of several generations, but in more than one respect presents a marked contrast to Egil's saga. It is less connected, confused in its chronology, obviously fictitious in a number of its details, and exhibits a late romantic tone which is at variance with the true saga-style. The latter feature is especially noticeable in what must be regarded as the central part of the story—that relating to Kjartan and Guðrún. This, however, is not reached till nearly the middle of the saga, which begins with the days of Harald the Fairhaired and the settlement of Iceland. Then it tells of Höskuld, a son of one of the settlers, who bought a bondmaid in Norway and took her out to Iceland with him. It was only when her son Ólaf was two years old, that Höskuld discovered she was really an Irish princess, whose name was Melkorka. When he grew up, Ólaf went to Ireland and visited his grandfather Myrkjartan (= Muircheartach in Irish), but returned to Iceland after the latter's death and finally took up his abode at Hjarðarholt in Laxdale. Then comes the account of Guðrún, daughter of Ósvífr, the fairest woman in Iceland, whose successive marriages left her still a young woman at the time when Ólaf's son, Kjartan, had grown to manhood. The story of these two really occupies but a small part of the saga, but its romantic character and its tragic ending make it stand out clear and distinct above everything else in the narrative. The situation is to a great extent the same as in the sagas of Gunnlaug and Björn, but is rendered much more striking by the strong character of Guðrún herself, compared with whom Helga and Oddný are weak and colourless. In the later part of the saga the defects in its composition become more marked; the fictitious element is very obvious, and defies all chronology. But while *Laxdœla* must in some respects be regarded more as a historical novel than history, there can be no question of its great merits as a saga, and it well deserves the high esteem in which it has been held in Iceland and which it has won in other countries.

Of a different type from these district and family sagas is that of Grettir the Strong, which, with the exception of a few chapters at the beginning and end, deals entirely with the life and fortunes of the famous outlaw, especially during the years from 1010 to 1031. In respect of his long outlawry Grettir was even more famous than Gísli, but his character is less attractive and his hard fate less touching, nor is it certain how far the saga can be accepted as giving a traditional account of the man and his exploits. It is clearly a pretty late work, written by an author of considerable skill, whose object probably was to compose a work of entertainment rather than of serious history. This enables him to invest his hero with a certain romantic interest; Grettir is distinguished above all by his strength and endurance, has a cheerful disposition in the midst of all his misfortunes, and is ever ready with a short and pithy proverb. The incidents which stand out most clearly in the saga, however, are mainly those which have no original connexion with Grettir, though it may be doubtful whether the author or popular tradition first brought them into relation with him. Chief among these is the tale of Glám, one of the most vivid and impressive ghost-stories in any mediæval literature. Considerable interest also attaches to the adventure with the troll-wife and the giant, in which there are obvious resemblances to the much earlier story of Beowulf and Grendel. The concluding chapters, which tell how Grettir was avenged in Constantinople, are also an adaptation of a common mediæval tale, part of which is found in the romance of Sir Tristrem. Even setting aside these episodes, however, the story of Grettir's adventures is interesting and varied, and the account of his later days in Drangey forms a fitting climax to the whole. On account of Grettir's wanderings during his nineteen years outlawry the saga touches upon many different parts of Iceland, and requires a considerable knowledge of Icelandic topography for the clear understanding of some parts of it. The verses, of which there are many in the saga, are mostly spurious and of little value.

The longest and the most famous of all these

sagas is that of Njál, which easily holds the place of pre-eminence among them, although critical investigations have shown that several serious charges may be made against it as a record of facts. In its existing form it is comparatively late, and is clearly a composite work, joined together with some skill, but showing distinctly the diverse materials out of which it has been built up. Although taking its name from Njál, it begins with a section, occupying more than a third of the whole work, in which the real hero is Gunnar of Hlíðarendi. It is commonly supposed that this portion represents an originally distinct *Gunnars saga*, which has probably been worked over and expanded by the insertion of fictitious adventures and spurious verses. Except for the personality of Njál, who plays the part of Gunnar's faithful friend and adviser, this section has no real unity with the main part of the saga, which begins with chapter 82. The subject of this is briefly the troubles which the sons of Njál brought upon themselves and their father, till in the end their numerous enemies, headed by Flosi, surprised and burned them all in their home at Bergthórshvol in the year 1011. Njál's son-in-law, Kári, succeeded in escaping from the fate which overtook the others, and the last third of the saga gives a full account of the steps taken by him and others to avenge the death of his kinsfolk. In the end Kári and Flosi were reconciled, and the story ends somewhat abruptly with the latter's disappearance at sea. Even in the two later sections of the saga there are portions which do not originally belong to it, and more or less interrupt the progress of the narrative. One of these is a full account of the introduction of Christianity into Iceland; another is a considerable portion of what must have been a *Brjáns saga*, or a history of the Irish king Brian Boru, who fought the battle of Clontarf against the Scandinavians in 1014. It is here that the famous poem is preserved which Gray paraphrased in his 'Fatal Sisters.' In addition to these, there are other minor passages which are probably late additions to the story, some of them giving impressive glimpses of supernatural occurrences; how far these were really believed in by the writer or his contemporaries, it is now impossible to decide. The process by which the saga as a whole was brought to its present form is also a mere matter of conjecture; it seems pretty certain, however, that the part of the saga relating to Njál and his sons is more original and of earlier date than that of which Gunnar is the hero.

Whatever the historical value of the story may be, Njál's saga stands unrivalled in several respects. The characters of all the leading persons, both men and women, are brought out with masterly skill, not by any attempt at description or analysis on the part of the writer, but by the simple account of their own

Part of *Njáls Saga* (chap. 124) from the oldest copy (MS. 2870) in the Royal Library, Copenhagen.

words and actions. Scenes like Gunnar's last defence in his house at Hlíðarendi, and the burning of Njál's homestead, have few parallels in Icelandic saga-writing; and in many of the minor episodes the author's skill is equally evident. The saga is also of great importance for the interest in legal matters which it everywhere displays, and for the light it consequently throws upon the history of Icelandic law. By its contents and style, as well as by its length, *Njála* is amply entitled to the place of honour which has been unanimously assigned to it among the sagas of famous Icelanders.

§ iii. *Ecclesiastical Sagas.* The formal acceptance of Christianity by the Icelandic community, in the year 1000 A.D., marked an important point in the history of the island, and its significance in this respect is fully recognized in many of the sagas. Although the new religion could not be expected to produce an immediate change in the character of the Icelanders, and to remove all at once the personal and family feuds which had marked the heathen period, its influence was not long in making itself felt in this direction. It is significant that of all the sagas which have been named in the two preceding sections, only a few relate entirely to events later than 1000, while by 1030 the material for saga-making had practically come to an end. For fully a century after this Iceland enjoyed a period of almost complete peace, and the minds of the leading men were largely directed towards the fresh interests introduced by the new faith. It is not surprising, therefore, that when Icelanders began to write down everything relating to their past history, they carefully collected the facts connected with the bringing of the Christian faith to their remote island, and then continued the history of the new religion to their own times. Even in Ari's *Íslendinga-bók* the ecclesiastical interest is strikingly predominant, more than half of the little book being given up to this theme. He relates with special fulness the introduction of Christianity and the names of the first bishops, and sketches the careers of the bishops Ísleif and Gizur, the former of whom died in 1080 and the latter in 1118.

The same ground is covered by the much fuller account in *Kristni saga*, which is partly based on Ari, but expanded by information from other sources. It opens with the story of how Thorvald the Widefaring and the bishop Friðrek vainly tried to convert the Icelanders, and then recounts the incidents connected with Thangbrand's highly militant missionary campaign, which also failed of attaining much success. The final efforts of Ólaf Tryggvason, and the notable scene at the Althingi, are then fully related; after this the work ends somewhat rapidly with matter copied from Ari relating to Ísleif and Gizur. A fuller and more original account of the mission of Friðrek is found in the short saga of Thorvald, which appears to be a translation of a Latin account by the monk Gunnlaug (*c.* 1200).

Of Ísleif and Gizur there are also accounts in the book called *Hungrvaka*, written about or soon after 1200, and so named by its author because he hoped that it might 'wake hunger' in its readers to know more about the great and pious men whose careers he relates. After the lives of these two there follow those of three later bishops, the last of whom died in 1176; all are told after the same model, in a simple unpretentious style, which together with the sensible preface gives a very favourable idea of the character of the author, whose personality is unknown. Where *Hungrvaka* ends, the ecclesiastical history is taken up by separate sagas of several bishops, three of whom held the older see of Skálholt in the south of Iceland, and other three that of Hólar in the north. The bishops of Skálholt thus commemorated are Thorlák († 1193), Pál († 1211), and Árni († 1298): those of Hólar are Jón († 1121), Guðmund († 1237) and Laurentius († 1331). The saga of Jón was originally written in Latin by Gunnlaug, a monk of Thingeyrar (see pp. 81—2), but is preserved in two Icelandic versions. Those of Thorlák, Pál, Guðmund, and Árni, are the work of contemporaries who were well acquainted with their respective careers; there are two forms of Thorlák's saga, and a later one of

Guðmund was written in Latin about 1345, but has come down only in an Icelandic translation. The life of Laurentius was written about 1350 by an intimate friend, Einar Hafliðason.

These lives of bishops (*Biskupa sögur*) vary greatly in interest and value according to the subject and the author; some of them contain many interesting passages, and excellent delineations of character, but their general effect is less attractive and their contents less distinctive than those of the sagas already dealt with. For the most part the narrative is drawn out to a greater length than the matter requires, and this diffuseness is apt to develope into tediousness and dulness. Hence the bulk of the *Biskupa sögur* is somewhat out of proportion to their merits, if they are compared with the best productions of Icelandic literature, but the lack of them would leave a serious gap in the history of the country.

§ iv. *Sagas of later times.* For about three-quarters of the eleventh century little is known of the civil history of Iceland beyond what can be learned from the lives of the bishops. In the twelfth century, however, a new period begins, represented by a steadily increasing saga-literature, which differs from that already described only in respect of relating to events of more recent date, so that the details are usually fuller and the legendary element almost entirely absent. The sagas covering this period, which extends from 1117 to 1284, have not all been preserved in their original form; some of them were at an early date employed in the formation of a composite work, now known by the title of *Sturlunga saga*, and are extant only as parts of that compilation. This collective work is so extensive (some 750 large octavo pages), and so full of complicated incidents, that it is impossible here to give more than the barest outline of its contents. The earliest portion is formed by a short saga of Thorgils and Hafliði, two chiefs in the north of Iceland, who fell out with each other and were only reconciled with great difficulty. The events related took place in the years 1117—21, and the saga contains some notable passages, such as the account of the wedding at Reykhólar referred to on p. 17, and an interesting scene at the Althingi. There is every likelihood that the author had personal knowledge of the events he records, though the date of composition may be thirty or more years later.

After this follows *Sturlu saga*, an account of some incidents in the life of Sturla Thórðarson, the father of Snorri the historian. This begins with the year 1148, and tells first of Sturla's quarrel with another chief, Einar Thorgilsson, which was ended in Sturla's favour by a regular battle in 1171. The later part of the saga relates to troubles between Sturla and Pál of Reykjaholt; these were finally settled by the interposition of one of the greatest men of the time,

Jón Loptsson, grandson of Sæmund Sigfússon, who also offered to take Snorri Sturluson in fosterage. As the result of this, Snorri was brought up at Oddi. The saga ends with a brief mention of Sturla's death in 1183, and was evidently written early in the next century by some one who had an intimate acquaintance with the facts and endeavoured to state them in an impartial manner.

The sections of *Sturlunga* which follow upon this have been compiled from three separate works. The first two of these are the sagas of Guðmund the Good and Guðmund the Dear. The former is an account of the career of Guðmund Arason (mainly from 1180) down to the time when he was elected bishop and set out on his voyage to Norway to be consecrated (1202). The compiler has here copied, with some abridgement, from the 'priest-saga' of Guðmund, the original and fuller form of which has been preserved and is printed among the *Biskupa sögur*. The other saga, not found elsewhere, deals with events which took place during the years 1184 to 1200, and takes its title (*Guðmundar saga dýra*) from a chief in Eyjafirth in the north of Iceland. Certain troubles rose out of a question of inheritance, and culminated in the burning of one of the parties in his house, a scene which is minutely described. The whole story anticipates the disorders of the coming Sturlung period, and loses part of its interest by the multiplicity of the details.

The main part of *Sturlunga* consists of the *Islendinga saga* written by Sturla Þórðarson (born 1214, died 1284), and commences with the death of the earlier Sturla in 1183. From 1203 to 1237 a considerable part of the narrative is concerned with Bishop Guðmund, with whom are also connected two independent sagas of some value. One of these is the saga of Hrafn Sveinbjörnsson, of Eyrr in Arnarfirth in the north-west of Iceland; this relates to a period extending from about 1190 to 1213. Hrafn is described in terms which recall heroes of the older time like Gunnar in Njál's saga; he was not only a good archer and athlete, but a skilled craftsman, leech, lawyer, and poet. In consequence of a vow, he went on a pilgrimage to Canterbury, and there offered to St Thomas the tusks of a walrus caught in Dýrafirth. Before returning to Iceland, he also visited the shrine of St Giles near Arles, and that of St James in Spain, and even went as far as Rome. At a later date (in 1202) he accompanied Guðmund, the bishop-elect, when the latter went to Norway for consecration. The voyage, which is fully described, was a very stormy one, and for some time the ship was in considerable danger among the Hebrides. The voyagers had also some trouble with Ólaf, the Norse king of the Hebrides, who tried to exact heavy anchorage-dues from them. In the later part of the saga the interest centres in dissensions which arose between

Hrafn and Thorvald Snorrason in Vatnsfirth, who finally came upon him unexpectedly, forced him out of his house by setting fire to it, and put him to death. This and some other events related in the saga were preceded by various dreams and portents, of which particulars are given with great minuteness. The author was evidently a contemporary and friend of Hrafn, and the saga must have been written not long after the latter's death; only the later part of it is copied into *Sturlunga*, the earlier parts of it have been preserved in the saga of Bishop Guðmund.

The other saga connected with Guðmund, but not included in *Sturlunga*, is that of Aron Hjörleifsson. Through a relative, who was a faithful adherent of the bishop, Aron was at an early age drawn into the conflict between Guðmund and Sighvat Sturluson, and took a prominent part in the fighting which went on in the year 1222. The attack made by the bishop's party on Hólar, and the return assault upon them in Grímsey, are extremely well told. After a gallant defence Aron succeeded in escaping, though severely wounded, and for some time wandered about, or remained in hiding, with occasional hair-breadth escapes. In the end he was able to reach Norway, and from there went on a pilgrimage to Jerusalem. On his return he attained to great favour with King Hákon, and had an opportunity of showing his generosity by rendering assistance to Thórð kakali, the brother of his greatest enemy, Sturla Sighvatsson. Twice he revisited Iceland, but ended his days in Norway (in 1255), and was honoured at his burial with a high encomium from the king himself. Of all these later sagas, that of Aron has most of the old spirit in it, and is less marred by superfluity of detail than any of the others.

The real *Islendinga saga* of Sturla may be said to fall into two parts, the first and shorter of which contains the events from 1202 to 1242, the year after the slaying of Snorri Sturluson. The second part, although much the longer, deals with a shorter period and ends with the year 1262. The interpolations in the first part have been already indicated; those in the second are even more extensive, and include sagas of Þórð kakali (1242—50), of the brothers of Svínafell (1248—52), and of Thorgils skarði (mainly 1252—58). It is thus a little difficult to decide how much of the collection is the genuine work of Sturla, and some have even held that only the first part is from his hand. Whatever the facts may be as to its constituent parts, *Sturlunga saga* as a whole is a work of great interest and value, both on historical and literary grounds. To appreciate and understand it fully, however, requires long and careful study, and it is only certain portions that can be read with the same enjoyment as most of the sagas relating to the earlier period. This is partly due to the blending of so many distinct narratives, by which the sequence of each is rendered less obvious, and partly to excess of detail, especially in respect of the number of persons named. From the historical point of view, however, this abundance of detail is a merit rather than a fault; and it is to a minute interest in persons and things that the greater part of Icelandic literature is directly due. On the literary side, *Sturlunga* serves to bring into prominence several defects which are really present in most of the Icelandic sagas, though in very varying degrees. One of these is a want of variety in the subjects; there is apt to be a sameness in the sources of the disputes, and in the fighting which arises out of them. The motives of action are often insufficiently explained; sometimes they are only to be discovered by observing closely the family relationship between the different persons. The task of keeping these clearly in the mind, and of distinguishing one person from another, is at times rendered difficult by the similarity of the names (as Thorgeir, Thorgrím, Thorgils). To these may be added the difficulties of genealogy and geography which have already been mentioned (p. 37). That in spite of these disadvantages so many of the Icelandic sagas must be recognized as works of exceptional merit is one of the strongest testimonies to the literary skill of their authors.

CHAPTER IV

HISTORICAL SAGAS RELATING TO NORWAY AND OTHER NORTHERN LANDS

In the first chapter some indication has been given of the continuous interest which the Icelandic settlers and their descendants maintained in the affairs of their old home-land, Norway, and of the way in which Icelanders who had been abroad were constantly bringing home news of what was taking place there and in other countries near at hand. When the practice of writing down the sagas arose, it was to be expected that all the information which had thus accumulated should receive attention, and as a matter of fact the saga-writers were as diligent in recording this foreign historical matter as in preserving the traditions of their own island. In this, as in other things, it was Ari Thorgilsson who led the way. The first version of his *Íslendinga-bók* contained 'lives of kings,' which he omitted in the abridgement. No doubt these accounts were very brief, and perhaps more chronological than historical, but it is clear that they served in some respects as a groundwork for later writers. These frequently cite Ari as their authority, and sometimes also quote his contemporary

Sæmund, whose views occasionally differed from those of his friend.

As we have seen in the previous chapter, all the sagas of early Icelanders are the work of unknown authors, and the same thing is true of much of the saga-writing which deals with the affairs of Norway. Here, however, the names of a few authors are known, and from the knowledge thus attainable it is easier to see how the work of making a full and continuous history of Norway was carried on. It was really a long process, effected only by degrees and with the help of the successive work done by a number of writers.

About the middle of the twelfth century lived Eirík Oddsson, of whom little is known except that he spent a good part of his life in Norway. He made use of his stay there to collect, from reliable authorities, information about the events of Norwegian history from 1130 onwards, and out of this he wrote a work which apparently came down to the death of King Ingi in 1161. This book, which for some unknown reason bore the name of *Hryggjarstykki* or 'back-piece,' has not come down in its original form, but parts of it are preserved in later works dealing with the same period. The names of some of Eirík's chief informants are recorded, and it is mentioned that in many cases they had been eyewitnesses of the events they described to him.

Somewhat later in the same century lived Karl Jónsson, who in 1169 became abbot of the monastery at Thingeyrar in the north of Iceland, but resigned that office in 1181, and went to Norway in 1185. There he attached himself to King Sverrir, and in consequence came to write the life of that ruler. In the prologue to the saga it is stated that a considerable part of it was written under Sverrir's own supervision, evidently the portion covering the years 1177 to 1184. The remainder (down to 1202) was derived from the accounts of reliable authorities, often eye-witnesses, and the work was no doubt completed in Iceland, to which Karl had returned; he was again abbot at Thingeyrar for some time, but resigned in 1207 and died in 1213. *Sverris saga* is a remarkably good piece of writing, and in the earlier portion there are clear traces of the king's own vigorous personality.

These two writers, Eirík and Karl, were thus dealing with events of contemporary history, in which tradition had no part to play. Others, however, directed their attention to matters of more ancient date, and endeavoured to collect the sagas of the earlier kings of Norway. Two of these were monks of Thingeyrar, Odd Snorrason and Gunnlaug Leifsson. The former of these wrote (about 1190) a life of King Ólaf Tryggvason in Latin; the original is lost, but there exists the greater part of an Icelandic translation made not long after the composition of the work itself. Odd's work is not a favourable specimen of the historical saga, being full of monkish tales and legends, uncritically accepted and unskilfully put together. He knew the work of Sæmund and Ari, however, and his own book was of some value to later writers. Gunnlaug, who died in 1218 or 1219, was probably younger than Odd; he was considered one of the most learned men of his time, and was especially a good Latin scholar. He also wrote a life of Ólaf Tryggvason, portions of which have been preserved in later compilations. His saga appears to have been much fuller, and better arranged, than that of Odd, but it is doubtful whether any higher place can be assigned to him as a historian.

While these are the only authors of the period who can be distinguished by name in this department of saga-writing, it is clear that before 1200 a number of other sagas relating to the kings of Norway had assumed a written form. The exact character of these cannot now be clearly made out, but it is obvious that the information they contained was largely utilized in subsequent works. Of one early saga, relating to King Ólaf the Saint, some fragments have accidentally been recovered, and show that it had considerable merit.

In contrast to these historical or legendary accounts of single kings, or of short periods in the history of

Norway, a desire soon manifested itself for a more continuous narrative on this theme. Ari's work may have helped to suggest the procedure, but the idea of a connected history of Norway, on the basis of the kings' lives, would very naturally have arisen in any case. More than one attempt to satisfy the desire was actually made. One of the earliest and briefest of these, now known by the name of *Ágrip* (compendium) *af Nóregs konunga sögum*, contains an account of the kings of Norway from Hálfdan the Black in the ninth century down to 1177. It is partly an abridgement of older sagas, and partly based on independent information, and was evidently written about 1190. The concise nature of the work excludes the possibility of great literary merit, and its historical value is somewhat unequal, but the author has taken pains with chronology, and shows an obvious interest in some aspects of popular tradition. On account of this, as well as by its early date, the compilation is of some importance.

A more ambitious work of the same kind is one that now goes under the name of *Fagrskinna* (fair skin), so called from the elegant binding of one of the two copies which existed in the seventeenth century: these have perished by fire (except a small fragment of one), but paper copies survive. This also begins with Hálfdan the Black and goes down to 1177; like *Ágrip*, it is partly founded on earlier writings and partly original. Throughout the work the author exhibits a special fondness for quoting old verses and poems, some of which are preserved nowhere else; the most valuable in this respect is the poem telling how King Eirík, who had fallen in battle, was received by Odin in Valhall. The narrative is full and free from digressions, and many of the more striking incidents are well related. The writer was obviously an Icelander, but it is also clear that the work was written in Norway; its date has been conjectured to be about 1230—40.

Another valuable compilation, probably a little earlier in date, is that contained in the manuscript known as *Morkinskinna* (rotten skin), which contains full accounts of the kings of Norway from Magnus the Good, and probably went down as far as 1177, but the end is now wanting. Its principal contents are thus the sagas of Magnus and of Harald harðráði, of Magnus berfœtt, and of Sigurd, who went as far as Jerusalem and so received the name of *Jórsala-fari*. The few other sagas it contains are much shorter and of minor interest. Throughout the work numerous verses are cited, and the text of these is remarkably good. *Morkinskinna* is also noteworthy for the number of short stories of Icelanders which are interpolated here and there in the course of the narrative, and sometimes interrupt rather awkwardly the sequence of events. In themselves, however, these *thættir*, as they are called (see p. 59), are of great interest, and many of them are excellently told.

About the same time that this collection was made, there was also written the most famous recension of the lives of Norwegian kings, that which now goes by the name of *Heimskringla*, from the words with which it commences. This was the work of Snorri Sturluson (1178—1241), and holds a unique place in Icelandic literature not only for its historical value but for its surpassing literary merit. In the prologue Snorri indicates the main sources upon which he relied— the statements of learned men, the poems of the skalds (see p. 11), and the writings of Ari Thorgilsson. He begins his narrative in prehistoric times with an account of Odin and the other gods, regarded as kings and chiefs, and then goes on with the line of the Ynglings at Uppsala, from whom the Norwegian royal line was believed to have descended. Throughout this section copious use is made of the old poem *Ynglinga-tal*, the author of which lived in the time of Harald the Fairhaired. Then follow the sagas of the successive kings of Norway, from Hálfdan the Black down to the fall of King Eystein in 1177. The majority of the sagas are comparatively short, the great exception being that of Ólaf Haraldsson (Ólaf the Saint), which takes up about three-eighths of the whole, and is sometimes found as a separate work. Of the others, the longest are those of Ólaf Tryggvason and Harald harðráði. But whether short or long, the sagas in Snorri's versions are distinguished by the utmost clearness in thought and expression. A sound historical sense enabled him to seize upon the essential points of the story, and to discard what was trivial or fictitious, while his skill in the use of language (an art which he had studied closely) gives his narrative a simplicity combined with precision and strength that is rare in the literature of any country.

Snorri's *Heimskringla* presents in a convenient form a connected, though condensed, history of Norway down to the year 1177. The further history of that country is related in *Sverris saga* already mentioned, and in an anonymous account of the events which took place from 1203 to 1217, troublous years during which the two factions of the Baglar and Birkibeinar warred with each other. During these years the young Hákon Hákonarson was growing up, and in 1217 began his long reign, which lasted down to 1263. It was in the latter year that Sturla Thórðarson, the son of Snorri's brother and author of the *Íslendinga saga* already mentioned, came to Norway. King Hákon had sailed on that expedition to Scotland from which he never returned, but Sturla gained great favour with his son and successor Magnus, and was subsequently commissioned by him to write the late king's life (see p. 18). This work, written within the next year or so, is both long and extremely minute in its details, while its historical accuracy is necessarily very great, as the events related were so recent and means of acquiring the best information abounded. The old saga-style, however, is still maintained, even to the insertion of verses by Sturla himself and by his brother Ólaf. At a later date Sturla also wrote the life of King Magnus, but only fragments of this remain; it forms the last saga of the Norwegian kings, and brought the history of Norway down to the year 1280. From Ari to Sturla there is thus a period of more than a century and a half, during which Icelanders were diligently committing to writing all that they could learn of the past and present history of Norway, and so succeeded in presenting an unbroken record covering more than four centuries, the greater part of which would otherwise be shrouded in obscurity.

Although the real composition of the older lives of Norwegian kings was over by 1230 or so, Icelandic scribes during the thirteenth and fourteenth centuries continued to work away at the materials already furnished, and especially to expand the original by insertions of various kinds. One of the latest and worst examples of this is the great Flatey-book, written towards the end of the fourteenth century, in which whole sagas are broken up for insertion here and there in the lives of the kings, so that the main narrative is often interrupted by a long series of such interpolations. In one respect the practice was a fortunate one ; it has been the means of preserving many pieces of saga-writing which are not found elsewhere in a separate form, and would probably have disappeared altogether if they had not been utilized in this manner.

One interesting saga which has thus been preserved in the Flatey-book is that relating to the Færöes (*Færeyinga saga*), which is mainly the story of Sigmund Brestisson and of his chief enemy and rival Thránd of Gata. Sigmund, who had spent the greater part of his early life in Norway, and was instrumental in bringing the Færöese to accept Christianity, was finally overcome by Thránd and his supporters, and was murdered on the beach of Suðrey, which he had reached by a remarkable feat of swimming. The remainder of the saga is chiefly a record of fighting and attempts at peace-making between the rival parties, and ends with the death of Thránd, some time after 1030. Although the traditions on which the saga is based must have been collected in the Færöes, or at least from men belonging to these islands, it is quite clear that the author was an Icelander, who probably composed the work about 1200. It appears to have been preserved in a fairly complete form, and has considerable literary merit ; some portions are evidently conventional fiction, but

Part of *Orkneyinga Saga* (chaps. 85–86) from the Flatey-book in the Royal Library, Copenhagen.

the greater part has all the marks of being genuine tradition.

Another saga copied into the Flatey-book, but found also in a separate form in other manuscripts, is that of the Orkney Earls (*Jarla saga* or *Orkneyinga saga*). This gives the history of the islands (and incidentally something of Scottish history) from the first coming of the Norsemen in the ninth century down to about the year 1160. The various sections differ in length and interest according to the personality of the earl they deal with, and the most important of these are Thorfinn, Rögnvald Brúsason, Magnus the Saint (killed in 1116) and Rögnvald kali. The account of the latter is very full and of great interest, as he was not only a man of many accomplishments (among other things a good skald) but had a striking career, and made a voyage to the Holy Land which is described with much detail. The saga, which is of great length, must have been written in Iceland about 1200, but the materials for it may have been gathered mainly in the Orkneys themselves, as Icelanders were frequent visitors to the islands, and Icelandic poets attached themselves to several of the earls. The mass of information contained in the saga, however, is a striking example of the zeal and diligence with which the Icelandic historians carried out their investigations, wherever it was possible to do so.

The only other northern country about which special sagas were composed was Denmark. The history of the early Danish kings, the descendants of Skjöld, was told in *Skjöldunga saga*, which was almost entirely of a legendary character; this existed as late as the seventeenth century, but is now known only in a Latin epitome. The later history, from Harald Gormsson in the tenth century down to about 1190, is contained in *Knytlinga saga*, a compilation which appears to date from the second half of the thirteenth century. Considerable parts of this were evidently derived from the works of previous writers, but a certain amount, especially in the later portion, must have been based on oral information. The lives of the earlier kings are treated very briefly, but the narrative becomes much fuller with the accession of Knút the Saint, who became king in 1080. In respect of historical accuracy the saga as a whole stands very high, and at times touches upon the history of England and other countries as well as that of Denmark.

A very remarkable saga relating partly to Denmark and partly to Norway is that of the vikings of Jómsborg (*Jómsvíkinga saga*), which exists in several versions. In its longer form there is a certain amount of introductory matter, relating to the kings Gorm and Harald; this has no real connexion with the proper subject of the saga, which is the foundation and history of the viking stronghold at Wollin in Pommern, ending in the unsuccessful attack made by the vikings upon Earl Hákon of Norway in the year 986 or 987. There is much in the saga that is fictitious or exaggerated, but the main outlines have a historical basis. Not a few Icelanders took part in the great battle in which Hákon crushed the vikings, and the subsequent traditions relating to this must have been based for the most part on their accounts, and on the verses composed by some of them. As a piece of story-telling *Jómsvíkinga saga* takes a high place, the account of the battle being particularly powerful and impressive.

The survey given in this chapter can convey only a slight idea of the great extent of the writings mentioned in it, and of the immense amount of historical matter they contain. Many of the separate sagas extend to hundreds of pages, and are full of precise details as to persons, places, and events. The more these are studied, the more marvellous it seems that such a mass of minute information could have been collected, remembered, and finally committed to writing, by men whose native land lay so far away from the countries in which the events had taken place.

CHAPTER V

MYTHICAL AND ROMANTIC SAGAS

As has been pointed out in the first chapter, saga-telling was employed in Iceland as a means of entertainment as well as of instruction, and for the former purpose fiction was as interesting as fact, or might even be received with greater favour by an ordinary audience. It is not surprising, then, that beside the sagas which are more or less based upon historic facts there also exist many which are mainly or entirely destitute of such a foundation. It is also natural that in the later period of saga-writing the number of these should greatly increase, for while historic persons and events were a subject which in the end could be exhausted, there were no such limits to the imagination of the inventive writer. Very soon, too, a knowledge of foreign romances came in, and opened up new possibilities in the realm of fiction, which were so diligently cultivated that this type of saga latterly threatened to supersede all historical writing.

A considerable number of these sagas, evidently representing one of the earliest types of Icelandic fiction, relate to persons belonging to the prehistoric period of Norway or the other Scandinavian countries.

To a certain extent they have a strong similarity to each other, most of them centring round some famous king or hero, who goes through a number of stock adventures, of which the commonest are combats with vikings, berserks, or giants, and the opening of grave-mounds in search of treasure. In most of them, however, there are more distinctive incidents, sometimes of a striking character, and often cleverly told. In the majority, too, the language is extremely good and idiomatic, and shows clearly that these sagas still belong to the classical period of Icelandic literature. There is every probability that most of them were written in the west of Iceland, where the literary tradition was strongest and best.

The close connexion between some of these sagas and the traditions of Icelandic families is illustrated by such examples as *Hálfs saga*, a loosely-strung narrative of which only a small part actually relates to King Hálf himself. His son, however, was the father of two prominent settlers in Iceland, from whom many distinguished men were descended. The disconnected character of the saga indicates pretty clearly that the writer was dealing with vague traditions, and the nature of these shows that fancy had played a considerable part in their formation. Thus King Hjörleif throws his spear at a troll or giant and strikes him in the eye; on a voyage he sees rising out of the sea a great hill shaped like a man and endowed with speech; there is brought to him a merman who can foretell the future, and so on. King Hálf, again, has a chosen band of warriors who are subject to strict regulations, probably modelled on those of the Jómsvikings. There is much verse in the saga, as in many of the others, and it is often difficult to decide whether this is older than the prose or is due to the same author. These verses are usually in one of the simpler metres, and in various ways recall the poems of the Edda; most of them express a spirit of manly daring which is well in keeping with the style of the stories themselves.

Other sagas which similarly link on with Icelandic genealogies are those of Ketil hæng, Grím loðinkinna, and Örvar-Odd, who represent three generations of one family. Of the three, the longest and most celebrated is *Örvar-Odds saga*, the hero of which was no doubt a real person, to whom all kinds of marvellous adventures are here attributed. In the beginning of the saga there is an interesting account of a witch, who foretells the fate of Odd, and his long story ends with the fulfilment of her prophecy. The fictitious character of the saga as a whole is perfectly obvious, and a number of Odd's adventures are of the most conventional kind, though not devoid of inventive power in the details.

The district of Sogn in the west of Norway is represented by a saga, that of Friðthjóf the bold, which has become very well known through the poetical version of it by the modern Swedish poet, Esaias Tegnér; of this poem a number of English translations have been made. The saga is mainly a love-story about Friðthjóf and Ingibjörg, and is attractively written, but has not the slightest historical value. There is much in it about a sanctuary sacred to the god Baldr, but there is little probability that this rests upon any real tradition. In the end Friðthjóf, who was only a yeoman's son, marries Ingibjörg, overcomes all his enemies, and has a long and prosperous reign.

It would be tedious to enumerate and describe all the other sagas of this type, which are commonly known under the title of *Fornaldarsögur,* or 'sagas of olden time,' and are sufficiently numerous to fill three substantial volumes (originally edited by Rafn in 1829—30, and reprinted with some changes in 1885—9). Two or three, however, are deserving of notice. The saga of *Hrólf kraki,* which relates to early Danish and Swedish history, is interesting for the old traditions which have been utilized in it, though its present form is clearly late and marked by interpolations. Here occurs the story of Böðvar bjarki, which has obvious relations with some portions of the Old English poem of *Béowulf*; also the famous visit of Hrólf to the Swedish king Aðils at Uppsala, and his strewing of Fýrisvellir with gold in order to delay his pursuers. The memory of another famous Dane is preserved in the saga of *Ragnar loðbrók*, so named from the shaggy trousers which he wore when he went to slay a monstrous snake. After various other exploits, Ragnar, who had succeeded his father as king in Denmark, ventured to invade England, but was defeated by King Ella and thrown into a serpent-pit, where he perished. His death was subsequently avenged by his sons, one of whom had obtained land in England by the old device of the bull's hide cut in strips, and thus became the founder of the town of London! A separate short piece about Ragnar's sons is more genuine than the saga in its present form. There is also a poem from the twelfth century (*Krákumál*), professing to be the death-song of Ragnar, in which his battles are enumerated and an ideal of dauntless courage finely expressed. This was one of the first pieces of 'Runic' poetry which became known in England, and ignorance of its real origin naturally caused much misunderstanding as to the general character of Old Northern skaldic verse.

There is also some remarkable poetry in the early part of *Hervarar saga*, which tells how Hervör, whose father Angantýr had fallen in battle in Sámsey, went to his grave-mound in order to recover the famous sword Tyrfing, which had been buried with him. The later part of the saga chiefly relates to Hervör's son, Heiðrek, and contains a curious contest in riddles between him and another person, who is Odin in disguise. There are echoes of real tradition in the saga, though the fictitious element is the predominant one.

In respect both of its contents and the mode of its composition *Völsunga saga* has a very distinctive character, which calls for special mention. Its main subject is an early form of the Nibelung legend, and it is chiefly based on a number of old poems, most of which are preserved in the collection known as the (poetic or elder) Edda. The author, however, had access to various other sources, written or traditional, and by a combination of these with the poems has succeeded in presenting a connected narrative stretching over several generations. The first personage of real importance in the story is King Völsung, from whose descendants the saga takes its name. These are especially the son of Völsung, Sigmund, and his sons, Sinfjötli and Sigurd. The latter, born after his father's death, is the hero of fully half of the saga; he is fostered by the smith Regin, kills the great dragon Fáfnir and becomes possessor of his hoarded gold, delivers Brynhild from her charmed sleep and plights his troth to her, is led by guile to marry Guðrún instead, helps Gunnar to become the husband of Brynhild, and finally falls a victim to her wrath at the deceit practised upon her. With his death, and that of Brynhild, the saga becomes the story of

Guðrún, who is next married to Atli, king of the Huns, and revenges on him the death of her brothers, from whom he had vainly tried to obtain the fatal hoard, now sunk in the Rhine. Still another marriage awaited her, and the closing chapters tell of her daughter Svanhild, trodden to death by horses, and of her sons slain in the act of revenging their sister. The whole story is skilfully pieced together, and told in a style not unworthy of the matter, mainly because the writer had the fine heroic poems on which to model his language; but credit must also be given to him for his ability to use them with judgement and restraint. Some passages may very well be interpolations, but on the whole the text has evidently been transmitted in much the same form as the author gave to it.

A very different version of the Nibelung story forms part of an extensive work entitled *Thiðriks saga*, which has for its chief hero the famous Dietrich of Bern, but includes many other legends which are but loosely connected with the main theme. A very interesting and valuable prologue states that this saga was derived from German poems and stories, which were recited and told in exactly the same form throughout the whole of Saxony. In all probability it was in Norway that these were learned from North German merchants, and there can be no doubt that it was an Icelander who wrote them down, some time in the thirteenth century. So voluminous and complicated is the saga that no detailed account of it can be given here; in addition to the whole story of Sigurd and the Niflungs, which is told with great fulness, it contains that of Velent (= Weland) the smith and his relations with King Nidung; there is also much about Attila both before and after his marriage with Grimhild. These and other episodes are so extensive that Thiðrik himself plays but a minor part throughout large portions of the saga. In spite of its interest in relation to German heroic legend, which it evidently reproduces with great faithfulness, the work as a whole tends to become a little tedious from lack of variety in the incidents; the description of fighting, between single combatants or armies, is especially carried to excess. The language, in marked contrast to *Völsunga saga*, is often of a rhetorical and inflated character, and clearly influenced by the style of foreign romances, though far from displaying the worst features of these.

In Norway, from at least 1225 or so, these romances had come into vogue under the patronage of King Hákon, at whose instance some, if not most, of the existing translations were made. He is expressly named as having commissioned the sagas of Tristram, translated in 1226 by 'Brother Robert,' of Elis and Rosamunda by the same hand, of Ivent (= Yvain), and of the mantle (*Möttuls saga*), as well as a translation of the *lais* of Marie of France. In addition to these, there are sagas of Erec, of Percival, of Bevis of Hamton, of Flovent, of Flores and Blancheflur, of Partalope, and some others. There is also a voluminous saga of Charlemagne (*Karlamagnús saga*), the result of combining a number of translations of French or Latin originals. These prose translations of Old French poems show considerable skill in adapting the foreign matter to Scandinavian circumstances and ideas, and as a rule avoid anything like servile and verbal reproduction of the originals. At the same time they introduced a style and spirit which were at variance with the best type of Icelandic saga-writing, but which rapidly came into favour in Iceland and had a pernicious influence. The great popularity of these romances, and of *Thiðriks saga*, was evidently responsible in a high degree for the decline in literary taste and in sobriety of judgement which becomes more and more marked after the close of the classical period. Their influence is also seen in a large number of sagas directly modelled upon them, which appear to have been written from about 1400 onwards, and are for the most part lifeless variations of a few conventional themes. As in the poorer specimens of *Fornaldarsögur*, single incidents or episodes may be fairly well told or exhibit some originality, but as a rule these sagas are merely tedious both in matter and in language. They were, however, extremely popular, and many of them were subsequently turned into metre, usually with elaborate rhymes; the sets of poems produced in this way are known in Icelandic by the name of *rímur*, and form in themselves an extensive and curious branch of literature.

There are two short sagas, of a different type from those just mentioned, which are worthy of brief notice. Both are sagas of travel, but in other respects they have little resemblance to each other. One is the saga of Yngvar the Wide-faring, a chief of Swedish origin, and tells of the strange adventures which he, and subsequently his son Svein, encountered in unknown regions of Russia. At the end there is a very circumstantial statement as to the authority for the story, but there can be little doubt that this is pure invention, and that the saga has no historical value. This is still more evident in that of Eirík the Wide-faring, who is represented to have been a son of Thránd, the first king of Thrándheim in Norway. One Yule eve he made a vow to go in search of that place "which heathen men call the immortal field, and Christians call the land of living men or Paradise." As the result of information which he obtained from the emperor at Constantinople, he was finally able to reach the earthly Paradise, where he remained for some time and received instruction from an angel. In the end he returned to Norway, but after living there for ten years he was suddenly taken away from this earth and seen no more. The story is obviously founded upon a few ideas current in the middle ages, and the lore both of the emperor and the angel is derived from very ordinary sources. There is some originality, however, in making an early Norwegian the hero of the tale.

In comparison with the immense body of fictitious literature relating to other countries, that which is directly connected with Iceland is small and unimportant. This is a natural result of the fact that the whole history of Iceland was well known, so that it was more difficult to find a place for what was obviously invented. In some cases the difficulty was surmounted by taking a real person of the saga-age, especially one about whom tradition had become rather vague, and treating his career in an imaginative fashion; some instances of this have already been mentioned in Chapter III. There are some sagas, however, which to all appearance do not possess even this slender foundation of fact, but are pure invention from beginning to end. Of this type is *Kjalnesinga saga*, the story of Búi from Kjalarnes and his son Jökul, whose mother was a daughter of the giant Dofri in Norway. With the exception of Búi's adventures in that country, the action takes place in Iceland and contains nothing improbable. In this respect it differs widely from *Bárðar saga*, which takes its name from a superhuman being connected with the great mountain Snæfell, and in which most of the leading characters are of a similar origin. In its own way this saga has some merit, and to a certain extent it is no doubt based upon local traditions and beliefs, but much of it may well be the product of the author's own fancy. A saga of another type, but connected with the same district, is that of Víglund and Ketilríð; this is in the main a love-story, and contains a number of verses which have quite a distinctive tone of their own about them. The brothers of Ketilríð try to throw obstacles in the way of her union with Víglund, but all ends happily at last. The story is simply and attractively told, and is obviously the work of a man of some taste and reading.

A saga with some original and entertaining features in it is that of Króka-Ref, who is represented as having belonged to Breiðifjörð in the west of Iceland. Having avenged his father and killed another man, Ref took refuge in Greenland, where he spent a number of years and had some stirring adventures. From there he went to Norway, although King Harald was unfavourably disposed towards him. By means of disguise and a false name he succeeded in evading the king's notice, and even informed him in person of having killed one of his followers; but the intimation was given in punning language which it took the king some time to puzzle out.

Subsequently Ref settled in Denmark and died in France, while on a pilgrimage to Rome. The story is pure invention, but rather well told, and the use of the punning speech is a novel incident.

One or two other sagas belonging to this class might be mentioned, such as that of Thórð hreða (which is of a plain matter-of-fact character), but they offer no distinctive features deserving of special notice. Those already described are sufficient to indicate the lines upon which the authors of fictitious sagas worked, and to show how persistent the Icelandic mind was in its desire to invent something new in the way of story-telling, even though the result was often little more than a new combination of the old and hackneyed themes.

CHAPTER VI

SAGAS FROM LATIN SOURCES

It has already been pointed out that the introduction of Christianity, bringing with it a certain amount of classical and mediæval book-learning, had much to do with the subsequent developments of Icelandic literature. In the classes of sagas already considered the influence of this foreign learning was mainly of an indirect character, serving as a stimulus, or occasionally as a source of information, rather than as a model for imitation. It was natural, however, that Icelanders who became good Latin scholars, and studied such works as were accessible to them, should very soon have thought of turning some of these into their own language. In fact, the practice of translating Latin works into Icelandic soon became extremely common, and a very large body of both secular and religious literature has been preserved in versions dating from the twelfth to the fourteenth century. In the best of these the native feeling for style is clearly exhibited; the translator does not attempt to render word for word or even sentence for sentence, but first of all grasps the sense of the passage and then retells it in his own way. Frequently his work is rather a paraphrase than a translation, with comment or explanation freely added wherever it seemed to be required. There are, however, varying degrees of merit in these translations, and some of them are sufficiently mechanical and even incorrect.

Among those which have been preserved, ancient history is represented by half-a-dozen works. The most comprehensive of these (now called *Veraldar saga*) is an account of the six ages of the world, mainly founded on Bæda's treatise. It gives a very rapid survey of the chief events of Jewish, Greek, and Roman history, and ends with a list of German emperors. Of these "Conrad was emperor when Gizur Hallsson was south," which pretty clearly indicates that the compilation of the work must be assigned to some time about 1200. Greek history is represented by sagas of Troy and of Alexander. The former of these (*Trójumanna saga*) is mainly a translation of Dares Phrygius, but with occasional use of other works. It begins with some account of Greek mythology and early legend, and ends with the reoccupation of Troy by the sons of Hector. *Alexanders saga* is a prose version of the *Alexandreis* of Philip Gautier of Châtillon, and was the work of the bishop Brand Jónsson, who died in 1264. The translation, which has much literary merit, was probably made at the instance of King Magnus Hákonsson, for whom Brand also compiled a history of the Jews (*Gyðinga saga*) from the rise of Antiochus to the death of Pilate. The earlier part of this is mainly based on the first book of Maccabees; the later portion is derived from various sources.

A fairly extensive account of Roman history (*Rómverja sögur*), which has partly been preserved in two recensions, is made up by combining translations of Sallust's *Jugurtha* and *Catiline* with an abridgement of Lucan's *Pharsalia*. The compiler was evidently well acquainted with Latin, and the Icelandic is remarkably good. This cannot be said of the remaining work which falls to be mentioned here, a translation of Geoffrey of Monmouth's history of the Britons (*Breta sögur*), in which there are many evidences of haste and imperfect understanding of the original. In one copy of this saga there is inserted a metrical version of Merlin's prophecies, which is known to have been the work of the monk Gunnlaug Leifsson.

Of far greater extent than the works just mentioned are those of a religious character, especially the lives of saints or holy persons. From an early date in Iceland, as in other countries, these were extensively read and studied, and were undoubtedly among the first things of which translations were attempted. This is indicated, among other evidence, by the fact that a considerable number of the very earliest specimens of Icelandic manuscripts (from about 1200) are fragments of these legends. Those which survive form a very extensive collection, which has been published under the titles of *Postola sögur* (one volume) and *Heilagra manna sögur* (two volumes); in addition to these there is a *Maríu saga*, accompanied by a large number of miracles. As these saints' lives form part of the common ecclesiastical literature of the middle ages, it is unnecessary to enter into details regarding the Icelandic versions. Of northern saints very few are represented, such as King Ólaf and his kinsman Hallvarð; the life of the former is mainly excerpted from Snorri's work, and that of the latter only survives in a small fragment. There is also a saga of St Magnus of the Orkneys, which is really an extract from *Orkneyinga saga*, but one version is interpolated with passages of little value translated from a Latin life, the author of which was a 'master Rodbert' otherwise unknown. English saints are represented by sagas of Edward the Confessor (*Játvarðar saga*), which is mainly a list of miracles, of Dunstan (compiled in the first half of the fourteenth century by Árni, son of the bishop Laurentius), and especially of the archbishop Thomas Becket. The latter are very extensive, and of one or more only fragments are preserved. Of the more complete texts, the older is of Norwegian origin, and is a translation of the *Quadrilogus* or *Historia quadripartita*. To Norway also belong the translations of the story of Barlaam and Josaphat, a work of considerable length, and of the Vision of Tundale (*Duggals leizla*). The former of these was made at the instance of King Hákon Hákonarson, probably about 1255.

Although these translated works have very little that is distinctively Icelandic about them, they cannot be altogether omitted in a general survey of Icelandic literature. They show very clearly the kind of reading which was most popular among those Icelanders who took an interest in the learning of the Church, and indicate the general character of the influence which might be exercised on the native literature from this source. The numerous lives of saints, with their long series of miracles performed by the more famous of them, undoubtedly gave suggestions for the similar accounts of Norwegian and Icelandic saints and bishops. The study of ancient history led to attempts to link on the early history of the North with that of classical and biblical antiquity, as is most clearly shown in the prologue to Snorri's Edda. This begins with the creation and the flood, the division of the world among Noah's sons, the tower of Babel, and so on; then it tells of Saturn and Jupiter, and other ancient deities, and of Troy and its kings. One of these had a son named Trór, "him we call Thór"; he married Sibil, "whom we call Sif," and from him Odin was descended. Odin left his own country, Tyrkland, and came north with a great multitude of people and much treasure. They first settled in Saxland, then in Jutland, and finally in Sweden and Norway; and from Odin the royal and noble families in these countries were ultimately sprung.

Fortunately this mode of applying scholastic learning is not at all prominent in the historical work of the best Icelandic writers, although it frequently appears in the fictitious sagas. It is well to remember, however, that such sources of knowledge were open to many authors during the whole of the saga-writing period, and would probably have exercised greater influence on the style and matter of the sagas if the art of these had not already been in a highly developed state.

CHAPTER VII

ENGLISH TRANSLATIONS AND OTHER AIDS

For the proper study of Old Icelandic literature a fair knowledge of several languages is essential, in order to read not only the texts themselves, but the best that has been written about them. It is possible, however, from translations and some other works, to make an extensive acquaintance with the sagas themselves, and with their history, without the study of foreign tongues. A considerable number of them have been translated into English, and most of these are of the kinds which best illustrate the different phases of old Scandinavian life in Iceland, Norway, or the British Isles. These translations vary much in respect of merit, and even the best of them leave something to be desired; there are certain difficulties in the way of converting the best Icelandic prose into equally good English, and the task of surmounting these successfully has not yet been accomplished. It is difficult, for example, to render neatly and yet clearly the many technical terms which occur frequently in the sagas, and to adapt the forms of Icelandic proper names so as to make them fit naturally into an English context. Some translators have adopted an archaic style, which has certain advantages and merits, but is too often carried to the verge of obscurity. The verses interspersed in some of the best sagas are also a great difficulty, and it is seldom that any serious attempt has been made to render them adequately. In the majority of cases, however, the translation is sufficiently accurate and readable, though it may fail to convey a just impression of the excellencies of the original. The prefatory matter to these translations frequently gives more or less complete information as to the externals of the saga—the sources of the text, the supposed date of its composition, its authenticity, possible authorship, and so on. It depends greatly on the date at which the translation was made, whether the information given on these heads can be accepted as reliable.

A general account of Icelandic literature, with much information on special points relating to texts and manuscripts, is to be found in the Prolegomena (of 214 pages) to the edition of *Sturlunga saga* by Dr Gudbrand Vigfusson, published at Oxford in 1878. In the second volume of this there is a large map of Iceland, as well as full indexes and various useful appendices. The same scholar, with the collaboration of

Prof. F. York Powell, also prepared the two volumes of *Origines Islandicae* (Oxford, 1905), containing "a collection of the more important sagas and other native writings relating to the settlement and early history of Iceland." In this work a large number of sagas and other texts are printed (but not always in full) and accompanied by an English translation; a few are given only in one or the other language. The account of the sources, and discussion of the value, of the various texts is very full and minute, but the views expressed are not always in agreement with the general opinion of other scholars. In some sections of the work the scattered evidence of the sagas on certain matters is brought together, as in that on "Primitive laws and customs of the days of the Settlement."

Of the five longer sagas of Icelanders the following separate translations are available. *The Story of Burnt Njal*, by Sir G. W. Dasent (1861, in two volumes; reprinted in one volume in 1900, and again in 'Everyman's Library,' 1912). *The Story of Grettir the Strong*, by E. Magnusson and W. Morris (1869). *The Eyrbiggia, or the Story of the Ere-Dwellers*, by the same, in vol. II. of the 'Saga Library,' published by B. Quaritch (1892). *The Saga of Egil Skallagrimsson*, by the Rev. W. C. Green (1893). *Laxdœla Saga*, by Muriel A. C. Press, in the 'Temple Classics' (1899); also *The Story of the Laxdalers*, by R. Proctor (1903).

Portions of *Eyrbyggja* and *Laxdœla* are also translated in *Origines Islandicae*.

The shorter sagas relating to Iceland are only partially represented by separate translations, of which the more important are the following. *The Story of Gísli the Outlaw*, by Sir G. W. Dasent (1866). *The Story of Víga-Glúm*, by Sir E. Head (1866). *Gunnlaugs saga* and the fictitious *Víglundar saga* are two of the *Three Northern Love Stories* by Magnusson and Morris (1875). The same translators, in the first volume of the 'Saga Library' (1891), have given the stories of *Howard the Halt*, the *Banded Men*, and *Hen Thorir*, while the second volume (1892) contains the story of the *Heath-Slayings* (i.e. *Heiðarvíga saga*). *Cormac's Saga* has been translated by W. Collingwood and J. Stefánsson. The sagas relating to the discovery of America by the Icelanders have been most fully dealt with by Arthur Reeves in the *Finding of Wineland the Good* (1890). Of the remaining short sagas, seven or eight are more or less fully translated in the *Origines*, together with a number of smaller tales and episodes.

Of the ecclesiastical sagas little has been translated outside of the *Origines*, which contains versions of *Kristni saga* and *Hungrvaka*, together with the lives of the bishops Jón, Pál, and Thorlák, and various smaller pieces and excerpts. *The Life of Laurence*,

Bishop of Hólar has been separately rendered by Prof. Elton (1890). The saga of St Magnus of Orkney is included in Sir G. Dasent's translation of the *Orkneyinga saga* (see below) and in the Rev. W. M. Metcalfe's *Lives of Scottish Saints* (1895). The Rolls edition of *Thomas saga erkibyskups*, by E. Magnusson (1875—83), is accompanied by a full translation.

The sagas of the kings of Norway have received considerable attention. In 1844 appeared *The Heimskringla, or Chronicle of the Kings of Norway*, by S. Laing (really translated from a Danish version); a revised edition of this, by R. M. Anderson, entitled *Snorro's Heimskringla, or the Sagas of the Norse Kings*, was published in 1889. A new translation from the original Icelandic, by Magnusson and Morris, forms volumes III. to VI. of the 'Saga Library' (1893—1905). Volumes I. and IV. of the 'Northern Library,' published by D. Nutt, contain *The Saga of King Olaf Tryggwason*, by the Rev. J. Sephton (1895), and *The Saga of King Sverrir of Norway*, by the same (1899); each of these forms a thick quarto volume. In the Rolls series there are translations of the fullest versions of *Hákonar saga* and *Orkneyinga saga*, by Sir G. Dasent (1894); the latter had previously been translated by Jón Hjaltalín and G. Goudie (1873). Volume II. of the 'Northern Library' contains *The tale of Thrond of Gate, commonly called Færeyinga saga*, by Prof. F. York Powell (1896).

Very few of the mythical and fictitious sagas are accessible in translations. *The Story of the Volsungs and Niblungs*, by Magnusson and Morris, appeared in 1870 (reprinted in the 'Camelot Series' in 1888). The saga of Frithiof is one of the *Three Northern Love Stories*, and has also been translated, along with that of Thorstein Víkingsson, by R. B. Anderson and J. Bjarnason (1877). The late *Ambales saga*, edited and translated by I. Gollancz, forms volume III. of the 'Northern Library' (1898).

In addition to the above, there are some works in which copious excerpts from the sagas are given, such as F. Metcalfe's *The Englishman and the Scandinavian* (1880) and P. du Chaillu's *Viking Age* (1889). A number of typical passages are also translated in *Stories from the Northern Sagas*, by A. F. Major and E. E. Speight (2nd ed., 1905), and *Translations from the Icelandic*, by the Rev. W. C. Green, in the 'King's Classics' (1908).

The fullest and most authoritative work on the sagas (and on the older Icelandic literature as a whole) is that written in Danish by Prof. Finnur Jónsson and entitled *Den oldnorske og oldislandske Litteraturs Historie* (in three volumes, published at Copenhagen, 1894—1902). The same author has also given a shorter account of the subject in a single volume in Danish (*Den islandske Litteraturs Historie*, Copenhagen, 1907), and on a similar scale in

Icelandic (*Bókmentasaga Islendinga*, Copenhagen, 1904—5). In German the sagas are fully dealt with in Chapter IX. of Prof. E. Mogk's article on Norwegian and Icelandic literature in the second volume of Paul's *Grundriss der germanischen Philologie*. In these works copious references to other sources of information will be found, the mere enumeration of which would sufficiently indicate the immense range of the subject in its widest aspects.

INDEX

Agriculture in Iceland, 43
Ágrip, etc., 83
Alexanders saga, 106
Althingi, 9, 38, 47, 70, 73
Angantýr, 96
Ari Thorgilsson, 21, 55, 58, 79, 85
Arnarfirth, 75
Aron Hjörleifsson, 76
Athelstan, king of England, 62
Attila (Atli), 98–9

Baglar (in Norway), 86
Baldr, the god, 95
Bandamanna saga, 59, 113
Bárðar saga, 102
Barlaam and Josaphat, 108
Beowulf, 66, 95
Bersi the fighter, 46
Birkibeinar (in Norway), 86
Biskupa sögur, 71–2, 74, 113
Bjarkamál, 51
Bjarnar saga, 49
Blund-Ketil, 55
Böðvar bjarki, 95
Borg (in Mýrar), 47, 62–3
Borgarfirth, 62
Brand Jónsson, bishop, 106
Breta sögur, 107
Brian Boru, 68
British Isles, 5, 8, 12
Brynhild, 97

Charlemagne, 100
Christianity in Iceland, 19, 23–4, 68–9
Clontarf, battle of, 22, 68
Constantinople, 8, 66

Denmark, 8, 90
Dietrich of Bern, 98–9
Drangey, 66
Drápur (encomia), 12
Droplaugarsona saga, 41
Dublin, Norse king of, 21
Dunstan, St, 108
Dýrafirth, 52, 75

Edda, poetic, 97
Edda, prose, 33, 109
Edward the Confessor, 108
Egils saga, 62–3, 112
Eirík Oddsson, 80
Eirík the Red, 24, 57–8
Eirík the Wide-faring, 101
Ella, king in England, 96
England, 47–8, 62, 96
Eyjafirth, 42–3
Eyrbyggja saga, 60, 112

Færeyinga saga, 88, 114
Færöes, the, 3, 88
Fáfnir, 97
Fagrskinna, 83

INDEX

Finnboga saga, 45
Flatey-book, 58, 87–9
Flóamanna saga, 58
Flokkar, 12
Flosi Þórðarson, 67
Fornaldarsögur, 95
Fóstbrœðra saga, 51, 57
Frey, the god, 38, 43
Friðrek, bishop, 70
Friðþjófs saga, 94–5
Fróðá, hauntings at, 61

Geoffrey of Monmouth, 107
Gísla saga Súrssonar, 52, 113
Gizur, bishop, 70-1
Gorm, king of Denmark, 3, 90
Greek emperor, 8, 17
Greenland, 14, 24, 51, 57–8, 103
Grettis saga, 65–6, 112
Grímsey, 76
Guðmund Arason, bishop, 71, 74–6
Guðmund the Dear, 74
Guðmund the Mighty, 43–4
Guðrún, d. of Gjúki, 97–8
Guðrún, d. of Osvífr, 22, 61, 64
Gull-Þóris saga, 53
Gunnar, s. of Gjúki, 97
Gunnar of Hlíðarendi, 67
Gunnlaug Leifsson, monk, 71, 81, 107
Gunnlaugs saga, 47, 113
Gyðinga saga, 106

Hafrsfirth, battle of, 3, 45
Hákon, earl, 91

Hákon, king, 18, 76, 86, 99, 108
Hálfdan the Black, 83
Hálfs saga, 93
Hall Þórarinsson, 22
Halldór Snorrason, 16
Hallfreðar saga, 48
Harald the Fairhaired, 3, 45, 62, 64, 85
Harald Gormsson, 90
Harald harðráði, 16, 84, 86
Harðar saga, 56-7
Haukadal, 22
Hávarðar saga, 55, 113
Hebrides, 3, 61, 75
Heiðrek, king, 96
Heilagra manna sögur, 107
Heimskringla, 11, 23, 85, 114
Helga the Fair, 47
Helgafell, 61
Hervarar saga, 96
Hlíðarendi, 67, 69
Hœnsa-Þóris saga, 55, 113
Hólar, 23, 71, 76
Horse-fighting, 43
Höskuld Dala-Kollsson, 64
Hrafn Önundarson, 47
Hrafn Sveinbjörnsson, 75
Hrafnkels saga, 38
Hrólfs saga kraka, 95
Hryggjarstykki, 80
Huldar saga, 18
Hungrvaka, 71
Hvalfirth, 56

Ingi, king, 80
Ingimund of Vatnsdal, 45

INDEX 119

Iona, 49
Ireland, 21, 47
Ísafirth, 55
Ísleif, bishop, 22, 70–1
Íslendinga-bók, 5, 24, 70, 79
Íslendinga saga, 75
Íslendinga sögur, 35

Jómsborg, 90
Jómsvíkinga saga, 90–91
Jón Loptsson, 73

Kári Sölmundarson, 15, 67
Karl Jónsson, abbot, 81
Karlamagnús saga, 100
Kjalnesinga saga, 102
Kjartan Ólafsson, 64
Knút the Saint, 90
Knytlinga saga, 90
Kormáks saga, 46, 113
Krákumál, 96
Kristni saga, 70
Króka-Refs saga, 103

Landnáma-bók, 5
Laws, writing of, 21
Laxdœla saga, 22, 63, 112
Leif Eiriksson, 57
Ljósvetninga saga, 42, 59
London, 96

Magnús Hákonarson, king, 18, 86–7, 106
Magnús the Saint, 89, 108, 114
Maríu saga, 107
Melkorka, 64

Merlin's prophecies, 107
Morkinskinna, 84
Myrkjartan, 64

Nibelung legend, 97–8
Njáls saga, 15, 67–9

Odd Snorrason, monk, 81
Oddi, 25, 74
Odin, 49, 84, 85
Ólaf Haraldsson (Olaf the Saint), 22, 51, 82, 85, 107
Ólaf Tryggvason, 48, 49, 70, 81, 86, 114
Olaf the White, 21
Origines Islandicae, 112
Orkneyinga saga, 89, 108, 114
Orkneys, 3, 12, 15, 21, 47, 89
Örvar-Odds saga, 94

Postola sögur, 107

Ragnars saga loðbrókar, 96
Regin the smith, 97
Reykdœla saga, 42
Reykhólar, 17, 73
Rímur, 101
Rögnvald kali, earl, 89
Runes, 19
Russia, 8, 101

Sæmund Sigfússon, 25, 73
Scotland, 21, 46, 62
Shetland, 3
Sigmund Brestisson, 88
Sigtrygg, king of Dublin, 15

INDEX

Sigurd, earl, 15
Sigurd, king, 84
Sigurd the Völsung, 97–99
Skálholt, 23, 71
Skarp-heðin, 15
Skjöldunga saga, 90
Sköfnung (a sword), 47
Snæfellsness, 60, 103
Snorri Sturluson, 11, 23, 33, 63, 73, 77, 85, 114
Snorri Thorgrímsson, 60
Stiklastað, battle of, 22, 51
Stúf the Blind, 12
Sturla (the elder), 73
Sturla the historian, 18, 75, 86–7
Sturlunga saga, 73–8, 111
Svarfdœla saga, 56
Sverrir, king, 17, 81
Sverris saga, 81, 86, 114
Sweden, 3, 47, 49

Teit Ísleifsson, 22, 24
Thættir (short stories), 59, 84
Thangbrand the priest, 23, 70
Thiðriks saga, 98–9
Thing (assembly), 9
Thingeyrar, 81
Thomas, the apostle, 50
Thomas, the archbishop, 75, 108
Thór, the god, 60
Thórðar saga, 49
Thorfinns saga karlsefnis, 57–8, 113
Thorgeir Hávarsson, 14, 51–2

Thorgils saga ok Hafliða, 73
Thorgrím Thorsteinsson, 52, 61
Thorgunna, 61
Thormóð Bersason, 14, 50–2
Thórólf of Mostr, 60
Thorskfirðinga saga, 53
Thorstein the Red, 21
Thorsteins saga hvíta, 39
Thorvalds saga viðförla, 70
Thralls, 6
Thránd of Gata, 88, 114
Trójumanna saga, 106
Tundale, vision of, 108
Tyrfing (a sword), 96

Uppsala, 3, 85, 95

Valla-Ljóts saga, 42
Vápnfirðinga saga, 40
Vatnsdæla saga, 44
Velent the smith, 99
Víga-Glúms saga, 43, 113
Víga-Skúta, 44
Víglundar saga, 103
Vikings, 2, 3, 5
Vinland, 57
Völsunga saga, 97

Weland the smith, 99

Ynglinga saga, 85
Yngvars saga viðförla, 101
York, 62